HUGO BALL
AND THE FATE OF THE UNIVERSE

Adventures in Sound Poetry

HUGO BALL

AND THE

FATE OF THE

UNIVERSE

by Lane Chasek

FAIR-MINDED FRAUD & FORGERY
A book series by Jokes Review

Copyright © 2020 Lane Chasek
All rights reserved.

Cover Art and Design by Mark Dwyer and Peter Clarke
Illustrations by Jack Roberts

ISBN: 9798646182419

jokesliteraryreview.com/books

CONTENTS

Preface   1

PART 1 – Hugo Ball: Sound Poetry's Stepfather
Genesis	5
Sound Poems	7
Hugo	10
Yes Yes Yes Yes Yes Yes Yes	15
Switzerland in Rotoscope	18
Masked Vigilante Justice, Pt. 1	19
Hugo Ball's Sermon	20
A Closer, Drunker Reading	24
Wordstuff	28
I Can't Find Him	29
News From Zurich	31
A Hidden Protagonist (potentially)	33
The Church Where We Last Saw Him	36
Corpse	39
Death of the Poet	40
Riddle #1	42

PART 2 – Resurrection is Temporary: Sound Poems, Entropy, and Randomness
The Random and the Temporary	45
Arbitrary Foliage on an Arbitrary Tree	46
Family History	49
Entropy and the Fate of Everything	52
Drunk on Entropy	54
Graveyard Shifts	56
A Voyage to Finland	58
Confessional	60
Translation	62
An Unnecessary Mining Allegory	64
Twins	66
Masked Vigilante Justice, Pt. 2	68

A Definition of Deus ex Machina	70
It's Not What, It's How and Why	75

PART 3 – God Was Nonsense Before He Was Jesus

Performance	81
How to Talk to Angels	84
The Final Name	86
Don't Read This Out Loud	88
Ghost in the Word	90
God in the Machine	92
Poetry as Prayer	94
Riddle #2	96

PART 4 – Scatland Utopia

Sweet Music	99
First Lady of Song	101
Synch, Pt. 1	104
A Séance	106
Scatman's World	109
Riddle #3	112

PART 5 – The World's Turning Like a Sundial

Synch, Pt. 2	115
Butterfly Bullet Without Wings	117
A New Definition of Trauma	120
The Saving Grace of Scattish	123
Childhood's End	125
Some Key Historical Events: 1916-2001	127
Masked Vigilante Justice, Pt. 3	130
It's Impossible to Be Completely Truthful	132

PART 6 – ----k-k-eee-yyyyyyfff

"I shall be reading poems that are meant to dispense with conventional language, no less, and to have done with it. Dada Johann Fuschgang Goethe, Dada Stendhal. Dada Dalai Lama, Buddha, Bible and Nietzsche. Dada m'dada. Dada mhm dada da."

– Hugo Ball

Preface

I recently turned my research into a lifestyle. It's a two-step process: First, abandon all sense of certainty in yourself, your language, the people you thought you knew, and history. Second, seclude yourself and tell any distractions you encounter they'd better fuck off quick if they know what's right. The resulting isolation will make it easier to read academic monograms, memoirs, journals, or listen to lectures by Noam Chomsky, Pentecostal prayer meetings, Ella Fitzgerald performing a duet with Mel Torme, or "Avocado Seed Soup Symphony." It all depends on what you're trying to learn.

In my case, I'm trying to learn sound poetry. I like sound poetry. I respect and get mildly aroused by sound poetry. It's the sort of thing I understand so well that I don't understand it at all.

So here I am, living a lifestyle of full-on research, so deep into learning about sound poetry I've totally stalled out. At one point, all I wanted was to write my own sound poem. Now here I am, so over my head in background noise I'm practically too paralyzed to breathe, let alone utter sounds I'd remotely call poetry.

Some poets insert themselves into their work so often

it should be a crime. Others are more elusive, hiding behind the third person or some collective "we." Some, like Ai, loved to write in the first person but only from the perspective of dead historical figures. Sound poets write without words, without grammar, without anything resembling sense, without themselves in any form. Their poetry is the poetry of corrupted hard drives, destroyed manuscripts, dead languages. They opt out of the language game completely. They're all at a party none of us were invited to, but I'm here anyway, trying to piece together their mother tongue. I'm secluded enough, ignorant enough now. I might be able to do it.

PART I

Hugo Ball: Sound Poetry's Stepfather

Genesis

This isn't the beginning of sound poetry. It's not even the beginning of Dada, Russian or Italian futurism, or scat singing. This is just one version of the truth.

In the beginning was the Word, and the Word was so lonely it created the universe. And in this universe existed a man and a woman. Their names aren't important. All you need to know is that the man and woman spoke a language that was basically the verbal equivalent of fucking. Every word they spoke felt like sex.

The Word, who'd created the whole shebang, was appropriately pleased. Sure, the universe was only temporary, but the Word had planned this from the beginning. Everything would collapse into a heap of ash and uranium in a few trillion years, but that was part of the fun.

Well, one day the woman was passing beneath a tree while the man foraged for nuts and berries. She decided to rest beneath this tree, and as she rested a serpent slithered down from the branches, rested its scaly body on the woman's shoulders, and began whispering to her.

"Archduke Franz Ferdinand was assassinated today," the serpent said.

This news distressed the woman.

"Russia's going to turn communist," the serpent said.

This distressed the woman even more. She didn't know what Russia or communism were, but they didn't sound good.

"Germany will have to pay reparations," the serpent said next, holding the "s" out for what felt like five minutes.

"You think that's bad?" the serpent said. "Hell, I haven't even gotten to the 1930s yet. That's when the really fucked up shit'll happen."

The woman woke up. The serpent slithered back up its tree and left the woman hyperventilating, her mouth suddenly producing sounds that had never existed before.

"My Word," she said, "what am I saying?"

Unlike the language she used to speak, this new tongue didn't feel like sex. It felt heavy and pregnant with too much meaning.

The man overheard the woman and abandoned his basket of nuts and berries to find her. He asked what she was saying. She said she didn't know.

The man began speaking like the woman. And they both forgot the language that had felt like fucking, and that afternoon they named each other. But their names aren't important. All you need to know is that the Word wept, then wondered why the hell it had ever given serpents the ability to speak.

This, of course, is just one version of the truth.

Sound Poems

You'll start hearing it soon. A gunshot echoing outside your apartment, dogs barking somewhere in a French novel, scat singing, languages that are born, die, or experience the terrible fate of having its speakers die off: all of these trace back to the phenomenon called sound poetry.
 It's meaningless noise, the literary equivalent of black-and-white snow on television. It holds hands with New Testament theology and the second law of thermodynamics one second then promptly tells them both to screw off the next. A poetic form born from the Dada movement (partially), it's exactly what you'd expect: chaotic, often juvenile, masturbatory, good-natured for the most part, and inclined to not give a shit (but only ironically). Deep down it really cares,. Sound poetry is concerned with the trajectory of our species and, in turn, our language. So it takes our languages, shatters them beyond recognition before the words we say and write have a chance to destroy us. It started with a man named Hugo Ball, but he was in no way the inventor of sound poetry. Think of him as sound poetry's custodian or doting stepfather.

Somewhere a dog barks at a flying bullet. Somewhere entropy is fucking up the collective shit of the universe little by little. Somewhere life springs into existence before going extinct five seconds later. Somewhere a drunk man falls asleep on his kitchen floor and babbles to himself like a baby and discovers he enjoys it. Somewhere a new weapon is invented. Somewhere a man convinces himself he becomes God by saying the right magic words. Somewhere Ella Fitzgerald's ghost is playing poker.

In the apartment directly below mine my neighbor argues with his girlfriend. The layers of carpet, lumber, and insulation mute any meaning their words might hold beyond the occasional "Fuck you!" or "How could you?" But the premise is there, along with the anger, the passion, the loathing. There may be some love there still. Their argument is slowly but surely becoming poetry.

Most human communication is nonverbal to begin with. Words don't require meaning, don't need to be signifiers to signify something profound. Somewhere between language and the sense we try to make of it is poetry. A sound poem just goes one step further.

Inspecting for Machine Consciousness

There's no point in writing a biography of Hugo Ball. At least not again. We already have Ball's diary, *Flight Out of Time*. But Ball wrote *Flight* with publication in mind, so everything contained in it is suspect. He probably makes himself look better than he actually was, but as far as I or anybody can tell, Ball's life was pretty boring when he wasn't performing at the Cabaret Voltaire. He mostly read philosophy, thought and wrote about philosophy, and speculated on what that philosophy meant not only for himself but the fate of his fellow Germans. He wanted the world to know not only himself but what he thought. If you look at the years between 1886, when Ball was born, and 1927, when he died, there's a lot that happened in the world, but it still only amounts to forty-one years of life. It's not much, but he tried his best to capture as many moments as possible.

That number, forty-one, might be important or it might not be. It happens to be prime, which is convenient. There's no pattern, no algorithm, nothing that can tell us whether a number is composite or prime, so the world's mathematicians have decided to agree that this makes prime numbers special.

Suppose you're working at a leather factory in your hometown of Pirmasens, Germany, like Hugo Ball, and you produce a large sheet of leather. Make a pretty 10x10 grid on it. Something like India ink or regular black paint will work just fine.

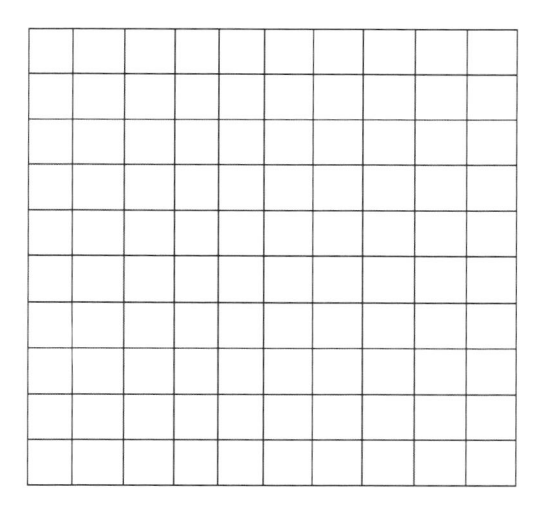

Great. Now, starting with the square in the top left corner, start counting from one to one hundred.

1	2	3	4	5	6	7	8	9	10
11	12	13	14	15	16	17	18	19	20
21	22	23	24	25	26	27	28	29	30
31	32	33	34	35	36	37	38	39	40
41	42	43	44	45	46	47	48	49	50
51	52	53	54	55	56	57	58	59	60
61	62	63	64	65	66	67	68	69	70
71	72	73	74	75	76	77	78	79	80
81	82	83	84	85	86	87	88	89	90
91	92	93	94	95	96	97	98	99	100

By this point, you should have already suffered your first mental breakdown of many if you're like Ball. Your father, a cobbler, has no idea that you spend most of your nights writing poems and plays when you're not working at the leather factory. You're just a working-class boy. How could anybody around you truly understand? But that's okay. Just ride out this breakdown and come back to this part later. When you're feeling better, shade in every number that's divisible by no other numbers but one and itself.

1	2	3	4	5	6	7	8	9	10
11	12	13	14	15	16	17	18	19	20
21	22	23	24	25	26	27	28	29	30
31	32	33	34	35	36	37	38	39	40
41	42	43	44	45	46	47	48	49	50
51	52	53	54	55	56	57	58	59	60
61	62	63	64	65	66	67	68	69	70
71	72	73	74	75	76	77	78	79	80
81	82	83	84	85	86	87	88	89	90
91	92	93	94	95	96	97	98	99	100

These numbers, whether prime or composite, mean nothing. But forty-one is there, a multiple of nothing but one and itself, the same way the interlocking histories of Germany, literature, and Catholicism had progressed up to 1886 to create Hugo Ball and shape him into what he eventually became.

Back to our hypothetical situation: Your parents will eventually get the idea to send you to university after your umpteenth mental breakdown at age twenty. Trust me, this'll be good for you. And in 1914, this guy, Archduke Franz Ferdinand, will be assassinated and Europe will find itself steeped in a war in which most men your age will be drafted, gassed, shot in the head, mentally scarred, crippled, killed, etc. You'll attempt to enlist three times, but the army will reject you, so you'll set your sights on becoming a pacifist artist and playwright. You'll flee to Switzerland, adopt the alias Wilibald, and form a creative partnership with a slightly older woman who dances and writes novels.. This woman, Emmy Hennings, will soon become your on-again, off-again girlfriend. You'll fall in love, popularize sound poetry, lay down the philosophical groundwork of Dada, retire to the countryside with your girlfriend, marry your girlfriend, and die the way prime numbers always die.

But most people will never remember you for your early involvement in German expressionism, your Dada manifesto, your dramas, both onstage and off. Just as death boils down to a single number, every life rounds out to a string of key events people love to remember. For Hugo Ball, these events were the creation of the Cabaret Voltaire in February 1916, a ragtag congregation of auteurs, performers, zealots, and pacifists of every breed from around the world who just couldn't fit into the violent machinations of Europe, not so much a locale but an event that created itself night after night from the ashes of wartime.

"The citizen is a commodity, too (for the state)," Ball wrote in *Flight Out of Time*.

And death is a number. What of it? If we have to be commodified, reduce ourselves to a single number or string of events, let's commodify and number ourselves in the way we want.

Hugo Ball's a commodity of history now, a commodity that serves as a lesson of life during wartime. Evading war, evading a neverending working-class existence, evading the trappings of grammar and lexicography to forge something so nonsensical it forced the world to rethink the meanings we've tried so hard to imprint on everything around us.

There are an infinite amount of prime numbers. But that's just one kind of infinity.

Yes Yes Yes Yes Yes Yes Yes

I once lived with a Bulgarian and managed to learn only one word of his language: Da (yes). Every time he spoke with his father on the phone, my roommate's responses would mostly consist of rapid-fire da's until sometimes he would sputter, "Dadadadadadada," for a full minute. Da is an amazing word, so easy on the mouth that it's often the first syllable a newborn utters. It's the perfect affirmative. Compared to the affirmatives of Chinese, English, French, and Lao, the affirmative shared by Bulgarian, Russian, Romanian, and other Slavic and Eastern European tongues perfected this expression.

Dada was supposedly named after this word, which is great to imagine. The legend goes like this: Marco Janco and Tristan Tzara, two Romanian artists, were already part of Ball's social group around the time Ball and Emmy Hennings were making their way through Zurich's art scene, and these two Romanians would constantly sputter "Da" at each other in conversation, probably because there was so much the two men agreed on.

Another myth (which is likely more bullshit than embellishment) involves Tzara eating a bowl of noodle soup in a parlor in Zurich. What kind of noodle soup he was eating doesn't matter. All that matters is that, according to this account, a murderer on the run from the law burst into the parlor, out of breath, begging for directions to a safe place he could stay. And Tzara, his mouth full of noodles and broth, pointed at a few doors, tried speaking with a full mouth, sometimes saying "Da, da," in a way his tablemates found hilarious. A refuge for the murderers, the adulterers, and the occasional saint. I really want this story to be true, but reality doesn't care what I want (unfortunately).

Hugo Ball wrote that the movement's name defies translation and etymology. In his own Dada manifesto, Ball wrote, "Dada is Yes. Yes in Romanian [and many other languages], rocking-horse and hobby-horse in French. For Germans, it is a sign of foolish naiveté, joy in procreation and preoccupation with the baby carriage."

He makes it sound like kid stuff, joyful lovemaking, procreation, and recreation, and that's the point of it all. Europe's young men were getting killed by mortar shells, mustard gas, trench foot, and the occasional stray bullet, and in Ball's mind this violence was the result of centuries of culture and language being used for evil on the continent. Art, language, all of Europe itself had all become too old and corrupted. Might as well start from the beginning, start speaking like newborns, and redeem ourselves and our language.

Dada loved African and Polynesian chants and sculptures. Dada loved collages of photographs, newspaper clippings, and schematics for alarm clocks. Dada loved nonsensical plays in which three performers, usually wearing garish masks, would all loudly recite their lines simultaneously. And Dada, of course, loved sound poems and poems that looked like pictures.

Dada spread like the idea of the steam engine, the Colt .45, mustard gas, or Spanish Influenza. It took off well enough in the German-speaking world, met an early death in France, influenced advertisers in the United States, and found a caring home in pre-WWII Japan under the name Mavo.

Dada is fully self-aware and knows it's being juvenile. It's not ashamed, though. Dada is no, Dada is hell no. Dada is yes, Dada is hell yes and hell no simultaneously. It's proud of what it does half the time and pretends to be ashamed for the other half, but only ironically. It's a child's playtime while people are getting their limbs blown off a few hundred miles away. This is the setting for Dada and the cradle of sound poetry.

Switzerland in Rotoscope

The right artists can give any neutral landscape a well-needed slathering of color.

Before arriving in Switzerland and settling in with his sometimes companion, sometimes lover Emmy Hennings, Ball had already dabbled in the German expressionism movement as a playwright and was now selling himself (artistically, not bodily) with Hennings to make ends meet in Zurich. He'd play piano pieces, ranging from classical numbers to popular ditties of the day, while Hennings made use of her experience as a dancer and chanteuse to entice the patrons of Zurich's bars into letting go of their hard-earned money. One gets the impression that Hennings was likely the breadwinner of the duo.

He had a taste of poverty, the elixir of deprivation every artist needs to test themselves with to see if this art thing is going to work out. Hugo Ball starved, but never to death. He wound up in jail a few times, but he made it out. And after all that, he still managed to found the Cabaret Voltaire and change the trajectory of poetic history.

Masked Vigilante Justice, Pt. 1

Early in the Dada movement, Hugo Ball and his cohorts donned handmade masks and started acting out nonsense dramas loaded with the fundamental truths of humanity. It involved God, it involved nonsense.
The scene:
You're one character out of millions. The world might end. You don't know this for sure, but it's a possibility. So you don a hideous mask and abandon your sense of self. You dance and sing in a language you've never heard before but understand perfectly. Do this alone, with a group of trusted friends, or with strangers. The results will be the same, just as they were for Ball, Hennings, Tzara, etc. Suddenly there are no young men dying in trenches or people getting killed by falling durians or coconuts in Thailand. Nobody's choking to death on a croissant, nobody slips on an ice cube and fractures their skull on their kitchen floor. All that's left is a group of bohemians tripping balls on futurist art and the primordial slime of poetry.

Hugo Ball's Sermon

Ball delivered his most famous sermon/poem on the same day my paternal grandfather was born in Casper, Wyoming. If my great grandfather hadn't emigrated from what is now the Czech Republic in 1906, then maybe my grandfather would have been born just a few hundred miles from where sound poetry was launched into the literary mainstream on June 23, 1916.

This could be significant or it may be coincidence. Similarly, there may be no thought at all behind Ball's sound poems or there may be hidden meanings we either choose to ignore or have given up on finding. But it's obvious that Ball wouldn't have given two fucks about what we thought. To him, rational thought was becoming the life killer, the mind killer, the body killer not only of Europe but the world. To kill this ultimate killer, Ball claimed to have invented "poems without words" (*Verse ohne Worte*) or simply sound poems (*Lautgedichte*).

Ball had to be carried onto the stage of the Cabaret Voltaire by two attendants that night. The garish cardboard outfit he'd donned not only limited his movement but also made him resemble a cross between an obelisk and a caricature of the pope.

Ball began his performance by reading some notes he'd brought along, notes about how language and poetry needed to be reclaimed from the modern world. Journalism and propaganda were partly to blame. Language's innocence, and thus poetry's innocence, had been torn away by years of abuse. Somebody had to invent a new language and methodology for the future of art and poetics, and Ball promised to deliver just that.

He read from three music stands, each carrying a poem. Each poem was nonsense but still carried an aftertaste of sense. He performed "Labadas Gesang an die Wolken," then held his audience in confusion and suspense with "Elefantenkarawane" (Elephant caravan). Then came the poem that would define the sound poetry of Hugo Ball: "Gadji beri bimba."

His nerves were about to get the best of him. He looked ridiculous, but that was part of what Dada was all about. The walls were black, the ceiling was blue. Terrible color choice, but what better way to speak to God or angels than by pretending a clear sky is above you while you're surrounded by darkness? But the idea that he was onto something divine wasn't what he feared. What he truly feared, I think, was messing up the reading, not putting enough soul or feeling into it. But then his voice took over. The moment or the poem possessed him. Or maybe it wasn't the moment or the poem but something else entirely.

"I noticed that my voice had no choice but to take on the ancient cadence of priestly lamentation, the style of liturgical singing that wails in the Catholic churches of East and West," Ball later wrote. Zurich was introduced to a new messenger of the meaningless and the inane, a costumed seeker of truth and beauty crying out to the world:

"gadji beri bimba glandridi laula lonni cadori gadjama
gramma berida bimbala glandri galassassa laulitalomini
gadji beri bin blassa glassala laula lonni cadorsu sassala bim
gadjama tuffm i zimzalla binban gligla wowolimai bin beri ban
o katalominai rhinozerossola hopsamen laulitalomini hoooo
gadjama rhinozerossola hopsamen
bluku terullala blaulala loooo"

    Something else may have been on stage with him. He couldn't see it. But it settled on his shoulders, slithered under his skin, into his skull, ignited his mind the way only a divine presence could. He continued:

"zimzim urullala zimzim urullala zimzim zanzibar zimzalla zam
elifantolim brussala bulomen brussala bulomen tromtata
velo da bang band affalo purzamai affalo purzamai lengado tor
gadjama bimbalo glandridi glassala zingtata pimpalo ögrögöööö viola laxato viola zimbrabim viola uli paluji malooo"

    The fictional priest mourned the dead youths of the village. Above Ball, above everybody in the Cabaret Voltaire that night, was a blue ceiling, which may or may not have transformed itself into a cloudless sky. But around them were still those black walls. Somewhere, somebody pictures outer space as black, others beige, others bright white. Blue wasn't a natural color though, Ball realized. Humans weren't natural. None of this was. What did space, the sky, or the earth think of humanity?

"tuffm im zimbrabim negramai bumbalo negramai bumbalo
    tuffm i zim
gadjama bimbala oo beri gadjama gaga di gadjama affalo pinx
gaga di bumbalo bumbalo gadjamen
gaga di bling blong
gaga blung"

Ball concluded his performance. Sweat-drenched, exhausted, the lights went out as soon as he finished. The timing of the lights, the words that had escaped his mouth, everything had gone off miraculously. He almost passed out as he was carried off the stage, a limp strip of man decked out in blue, red, and gold cardboard.

A Closer, Drunker Reading

This project is only going to get more cumbersome. I've acted as commentator, historian, biographer, bullshitter, math teacher, and now I'm adding critic and translator to the list.

My interpretation of "Gadji beri bimba" may be close to what Ball intended, or it may miss the point entirely. Maybe there was no point to begin with and trying to find one is missing a metapoint. Who knows.

Repeated sounds seem like a good place to start. This is a sound poem, after all. In the first stanza, Ball begins a lot of lines with some sort of "gadj-" sound, either in the form of "gadji" or "gadjama." These repeated sounds invoke an imaginary language, and these "gadj-" words could be the declension of a noun or a verb in different tenses. In either case, we at least know these words share some kind of connection. I don't know what else to say about them, though, other than that there's a connection.

Now that some of the sounds are out of the way, let's look at the verses and how they function. The first three verses all begin with some variation of "gadj-" followed by what sounds like a parody of a Latin High Mass, which isn't surprising. Ball was raised Catholic and even returned to the Church after his Dada phase. So are these lines meant as parody? Or are they meant to put the audience in the state of mind of somebody listening to a Catholic Mass? It doesn't matter since Ball's cardboard costume and choice of sounds work wonders: we're in a make-believe land where nonsense is Latin and a man dressed in cardboard is a priest. Whether sincere or ironic, imitation and imagination create an echo of meaning in meaninglessness.

And here's where I got lazy and started to give up in frustration and intoxication. That "o" that begins the fifth line might suggest the speaker is addressing somebody or uttering a lamentation, but fuck if I know. The poem is building up energy, though, that's what matters. Notice how Ball's using more "z" sounds, keeping the listener/reader zipping through the lines. And what's with "rhino-" appearing so many times? This prefix signifies that noses are somehow involved, and of course it makes me think of rhinoceroses or maybe even elephants, since elephants have pretty big noses.

And now we come to the second stanza. More "z" sounds, more speed. What the hell is going on? Speed, that's what. Also, look at that, right there on the second line: "elifantolem." Yep, some kind of elephant is involved. This isn't Ball's poem about an elephant caravan, but maybe Ball was just really into elephants. Also, "ögrögöööö" sounds like it could be an onomatopoeia. My guess is that the elephant is eating. Not just eating but eating in a way that would make a mortal human shit their pants in terror. It certainly doesn't look like any normal human-produced sound I've ever seen on paper.

Final stanza: we're almost at the finish line and I'm almost out of beer. I'm starting to enjoy this. A lot of "gadj-" words again. Makes sense. Even a sound poem needs a sense of closure, a sense of swallowing its own tail to form a perfect circle. But what's this? "Gaga." Also, the final verses are shrinking. The speaker's tongue slows down, starts stumbling around the awkwardness of the "g" sounds. "Bling blong" and "blung" almost read like a question and answer sequence. It is what it is. An open-and-shut case. Take it or leave it. End of poem.

So what does it all mean?

Well, it's about an elephant. But not just any elephant. This is a Jupiter-sized elephant that drifts through the galaxy in search of planets to crack open and devour like peanuts. And this elephant drifts into our solar system, finds this planet called Earth, and notices that a bunch of little animals on this planet are bombing and gassing each other, lighting shit on fire, clubbing baby seals in Canada, and wearing socks with sandals. Some really ghastly, fucked shit. So what does this elephant do? It brings about Judgment Day. But this Judgment Day has no God or Satan, no singing angels, no divine numerology, no sheep or goats, no rising of the dead, no ascension of nude bodies and planets crumbling into brimstone. This Judgment Day consists of a hungry Jupiter-sized elephant taking hold of our planet with its trunk and popping it in its hungry maw like a peanut. That "ögrögöööö" is the elephant satisfying its hunger and punishing us for our sins. And that's what the priest in the poem is trying to tell us. He isn't warning us about the elephant, he's just reminding us that the elephant will drift by someday.

Wordstuff

Dada and Ball's work found their way to Eastern Europe and settled in the minds of a few Czech artists in Prague. Some embraced it right away. Others embraced it only to abandon it a few months later.

In a 1922 issue of *Ma*, the Czech literary journal of Dada, Dragan Aleksić published "Taba Ciklon II," a sound poem which pissed off so many of his friends that he became an artistic pariah in his own city. Compared to Ball's work in the genre, Aleksić's poetry is playful and pokes fun at the very idea of sound poetry. "Taba Ciklon II," as far as I can tell, tries to imitate an internal combustion engine revving up, which may have been Aleksić's way of commenting on the rise of the machine age in Europe, but he soon unravels that possibility by ending the poem with the phrase "parlevufranse," as if the poem's speaker is asking the reader if they can speak French or any language, it doesn't matter which. The poem grasps at a real language it can cling to and unravels its own genre.

Aleksić's former comrades were through with this cutesy, primitivist shit. To many, the kidstuff of Dada was more annoying than endearing as time wore on.

I Can't Find Him

The man I'm trying to find, Hide Kinoshita, is nowhere to be found. I want his story, want to twist and retell it, but it's like his ghost has caught word of what I'm trying to write, so now he's trying to throw me off his trail. Even his romanized name suggests he's hiding or reminding himself to hide, even though he's a glowing example of just how far-reaching Ball's influence was.

A man descends into a bathtub dressed in a black dress shirt, slacks, and the black socks you see people wearing at funerals. He exclaims something that may or may not be inspired by the Japanese language. He retrieves a miniature gong from a rubber bath mat, strikes it, then lowers the gong into the water. The gong's voice mutates into something more than gong, more than water.

He finds a plastic tube from that same rubber mat, rotates it and marvels at the quacking noise it produces. Another turn and it mews like a disturbed kitten. Cue a record scratch. Rising from the water, his shirt and slacks completely drenched, he babbles something either to himself or to all of us, cues another record scratch, imitates

Donald Duck, clicks his tongue. Running his wet hands across the walls of the bathroom, he produces a beautiful squawking sound and revels in the symphony he's creating in isolation. "Isolation itself has become an artform," Hugo Ball once wrote. We're witnessing this theory's application.

This man is Adachi Tomomi, performing a sound poem titled "Voice Sound Poetry Form Begun with -X-" published by Hide Kinoshita in 1924. Think of Tomomi as a cross between Edgar Winters and the mad scientist from *The Brain that Wouldn't Die*. His specialty is performing poems like Kinoshita's. He even composes a lot of his own. You can check him out sometime on your own, but all I want right now is the original source, Kinoshita himself, and his reluctance to reveal himself is making it very difficult to write about him.

Kinoshita, I've sought you for so long. Are you angry? I try Googling your name and I can only find sentence-long biographies about your work and inspirations. I try looking up photographs of you and all I find are pictures of brown-haired anime girls in school uniforms. What are you trying to tell me?

Sometimes ghosts just want to be left alone. The dead can be stubborn.

News from Zurich

Hugo Ball's Dada manifesto marked the end of his involvement with Dada. When he read it during one soirée in 1917, it was an unofficial announcement that he and Hennings were moving on. The scene had gotten too hectic and too stale at the same time. So if you're tired of hearing about Dada, good news: the story's almost over.

I won't bore you with details of what Ball wanted from Dada. Chances are he just wanted some outlet. Here he was, stranded in a strange land, the oldest man in his friend group by at least eight years with a reputation for being too stern, too stoic, too much like a socially awkward priest rather than a musician, poet, or playwright. He'd dabbled in drama, music, live variety-shows and micless open-mic nights of all shapes and dimensions. He wanted to remove himself, Hennings, and Hennings' tween daughter from a previous marriage to the Alps to reflect on poetry, religion, and the future of the two disciplines.

Or maybe Ball was on the verge of losing everything mentally and emotionally. He'd already had a history of mental breakdowns in Germany before attending university, and after witnessing the battlefields of Belgium in

1914 (as a spectator only), getting thrown in prison once he'd arrived in Switzerland, living on a meager combination of love and poverty before breaking through with the Cabaret Voltaire, he probably wondered if city life was worth it anymore.

And romantic troubles. I can't forget about romantic troubles. I wrote earlier that Ball and Hennings began their relationship as working companions rather than lovers. Well, it wasn't until they moved out of Zurich that Hennings finally decided to settle down with Ball and Ball alone, and Ball was probably consumed with jealousy up until that point. There's only so much frustration a man can take in a few years.

During the height of the Cabaret's lifetime, Hennings had started seeing a Spanish journalist. They'd taken a liking to each other, so Hennings started taking this young man around Zurich on dates, all while Ball followed them over the course of several days with a loaded pistol. But "followed" isn't the right word. What Ball was doing was really stalking and threatening to kill a woman he wanted desperately to claim as his own in a land that would never be his own, all while taking part in the creation of a new artistic culture he felt too old for.

He never mentions stalking Hennings with a deadly weapon in *Flight out of Time*. Maybe he wrote about it once but felt too ashamed to publish it, but time has a habit of bringing those episodes to light.

A Hidden Protagonist (Potentially)

I'd like to imagine a series of events in which Ball was just a footnote to Hennings' life instead of the other way around, but I realize this is impossible. The early 20th century still called for a man to be the protagonist of any drama, while Hennings was the love interest. Hennings, meanwhile, got cast as the angel, the dancer, or the showgirl of Dada.

We don't need to look any further than a 1917 Dada soirée, which featured the performance of Oskar Kokoschka's *Sphinx and Strawman*. Hugo Ball gets top billing as the masked Mr. Firdusi, while Hennings plays the roles of "Female Soul, Anima," a feminine abstraction.

In August of that same year, Emmy Hennings read a story publicly, more of a vignette, titled "Kritik der Leiche." It's bad form to read too much of a writer's life into their work, but you can't help but wonder if the corpse is actually Hennings voicing her complaints to Ball. She and Ball would be married soon, but who would have imagined it at the time?

"You might not have known that I'm a corpse," the narrator of the story states. The corpse addresses an unspecified "you," some "dear sir." The corpse speaks to a man, though the corpse could be a man, a woman, neither, or both.

I've dedicated so much time and energy to quoting Hugo Ball, using his words as a kind of secondhand insight into the inner workings of the mind of a sound poet. But there were poets beside Ball, several figures he overshadowed for no reason other than the fact that he was a man and some of those figures (such as Hennings) were women.

Ball died a prime number, forty-one. Nothing about him could be replicated, and I confess now that I'm quoting a corpse. Hennings is a corpse, too, but her corpse is fresher since she didn't die until 1948 (which isn't prime), when she was sixty-three (also not prime). But there's a significance to her death, just as there's a significance to Ball's death.

"My death has been fruitless," Hennings' corpse declares. What death has ever been fruitful, though?

"It's in the very essence of my corpse to demand rest," the corpse says. Every spirit, every animated, rotting body on the planet in every story of the supernatural ever told seems to seek the same thing: rest. But where can you go after you rest? What happens to the ghost after its purpose is fulfilled?

There needs to be a meaning to death. At least, that's what most people want. Since Ball witnessed the Belgian front in 1914 after failing three times to enlist in the German army, I imagine Ball desperately craved a slice of that action, that release of death that would be just one metaphorical dice roll away from stealing away his life and the future of Dada and sound poetry with him. Maybe he would have died at twenty, twenty-one, or twenty-two instead of forty-one. How inconvenient for me. But he lived, he loved, he married, he created, and he overshadowed.

"I will live," the corpse states toward the end of Hennings' story. "I'm not dead because I'm not resting. I think: I live."

The Church Where We Last Saw Him

Hugo Ball retired to Catholicism and the countryside, a much-needed exile after the hectic, secular pace of Zurich, Dada, and WWI. Ball, Hennings, and Henning's daughter settled into their new lives, Dada now nothing more than a fad, like bellbottom jeans or flower power.

Actually, that isn't true. If you're looking for the true story of Hugo Ball, this isn't it. For a man who lived so briefly, there was no chance of him ever retiring. In seclusion, Ball's writing took a bend toward the spiritual and political, two areas that were already closely connected in his mind. Ball settled into Dada for the rest of his life without realizing it. Or maybe "settled" isn't the right word. He tried to overcome it, abandoning sound poetry and nonsense plays for the comforts of political treatises, but it was still Dada in essence, just a more grown-up, pissed-off version of the movement.

The German-speaking world was in trouble according to Ball. Too bellicose, not enough spirit, not enough childlike wonder: no wonder Germania was headed down the wrong path. For centuries Germany had been the world's edgy, contrarian high schooler who thought existentialism and material gain were philosophy's final acts. Materialism was one problem, but even worse to Ball was the need to participate in wars (both literal and metaphorical) against everybody and everything. Whether it was a series of worldwide wars or the Protestant Reformation, the German mindset had found a way to create and engage in conflicts for the sake of creating and sustaining conflicts.

What was the world supposed to learn from the Great War? What were we supposed to learn from Dada? Was protest enough? Ball doubted it was.

"I have examined myself carefully," he wrote while still in Zurich. Supposedly. Keep in mind that Ball published *Flight Out of Time* long after he quit the Dada scene, so everything he writes is suspect, the thoughts of an older, more reflective Ball. "I could never bid chaos welcome, throw bombs, blow up bridges, and do away with ideas. I am not an anarchist. The longer and farther I am away from Germany, the less I am likely to be one."

Protest had consumed his life for far too long and had consumed Europe's for too long as well.

In 1517, Martin Luther created Protestantism out of nothing more than a quill, some paper, a dash of moral fury, and a nail long and sharp enough to append his theses to the door of a cathedral. Protest, pure and simple. Even the name suggests a religion founded on protest and dissent. It's not the kind of protest you'd find in a Woody Guthrie song, but a purer, more distilled species of protest, and now Europe's artists were echoing Luther's actions centuries later.

Ball wanted out of it all. He wanted out of protest, even though he'd helped found a movement founded on protest. He wanted out of poetry and theatre. He wanted out of Dada. He wanted out of Germany, both the country and its people. The German-speaking world already hated him for what he'd written about his fellow countrymen and women, and now he'd started writing against the branch of Christianity that Germany had created.

The world's artists couldn't protest forever. Once art goaded the world into solving all its problems, what use would protest art have? When it does its job too well, the art of protest destroys itself. Better to stick to the security blanket of the One-And-Only, Holy, Apostolic Catholic Church, the status quo, the golden ratio, the universal mean, God, whatever you want to call it. That's what Ball eventually settled on.

Corpse

A dead body protests its own decomposition. Its organs, identity, and mind used to be part of a very specialized, specific order and set of functions, but now that order is lost. Temporarily, the corpse's condition is no different from the lives of any living thing. Timing and nomenclature are really the only differences between life and death. Every living thing is dying. The corpse in question has just crossed that imaginary, arbitrary line somebody decided to call "death." Now thermodynamics' second and deadliest law comes at life with its full arsenal.

There will no longer be time for Spanish lovers, excursions into the Alps, histories on Byzantine Christianity, or even speculating on the linguistic aspects of the Deity. Dada no longer acts as sound poetry's cradle but sound poetry's (sometimes) supportive stepfather.

Hugo Ball and Emmy Hennings remain corpses as I type this. They, too, know entropy.

Death of the Poet

You may not need translators for sound poems, but interpreters help. A Brazilian sound poem will sound radically different from a German or Japanese sound poem. Despite their best efforts to shake free of the phonetic and grammatical rules of their mother tongue, a sound poet's work will bear the flavor of Portuguese, German, Japanese, or whatever language they grew up with.

A weakness of our own minds? Maybe. But this weakness makes the realm of sound poetry the most democratic literature in the world. Forget death of the author. Sound poetry kills both author and reader, then resurrects them into the same persona. There's no meaning to the poem, at least no meaning beyond the fact that there is no meaning, so the poet's interpretation of their work becomes no more valid than any one reader's interpretation. Consensus becomes impossible. There's no right or wrong, not even a general sense of rightness or wrongness. All you have are people debating over the body of a language that was never born. This language could be the language of angels or it could be the language chinchillas would have developed if they'd gained sentience. There's possibility, suggestions of alternate histories and languages, but none of them can be grasped by the poet or the reader. We're outside that alternate world, ghosts drifting through the ghost of a stillborn language.

Riddle #1

Q: What's the difference between boredom and freedom?

A: The country you live in, the size of your genitalia, etc., etc.

PART II

Resurrection Is Temporary:
Sound Poems, Entropy, and Randomness

The Random and the Temporary

"You never stand in the same river twice," a painter named Jonathan Hale once told me. He was explaining his painting "Heraclitus Unbounded" to me, named after a Greek philosopher known for his bouts of crying, hand-wringing, and constant worrying about mortality and the fate of the human soul.

According to Hale, Heraclitus wasn't the first philosopher to be credited with this saying. It was a common thought that struck upon the ever-shifting, chaotic world around us since time immemorial. An ever-moving entity, a river at any one spot will be filled with different water, different sediments, different minnows and tadpoles on a moment-to-moment basis. So if you ever decide to visit the creek or river where you once fished or skinny-dipped when you were younger, you'll never be able to relive it. Not completely. Just as the cells, atoms, and molecules in our body are replaced every ten years or so, so too is the river subject to the same gradual replacement. There's nothing inherently special about this moment's river or the next moment's river, or this decade's you or the next decade's you. Life is horrifying but also inspiring that way.

Arbitrary Foliage on an Arbitrary Tree

The Swiss had everything in the 1910s. They weren't involved in any wars, for starters, so every pacifist, artist, troubled philosopher, scared scientist, bohemian, and most other species of conscientious objector flocked there like war-opposing flies to a peaceful slice of cinnamon butterscotch pie. Add to that the wonders of Swiss banking and an abundance of quality watches, ski slopes, and pastries and you have the perfect conditions for attracting and holding onto fresh talent in Zurich and fostering new artistic movements, philosophical schools, and scientific theories. Wartime is always a good time for the Swiss and WWI was no exception.

But even before Franz Ferdinand was assassinated and world history took a nosedive into self-destruction, one of the world's most famous linguistic revolutionaries had lived and died in Switzerland virtually unnoticed. Coincidentally (or fortuitously), this man was also named Ferdinand, Ferdinand de Saussure. Unlike Hugo Ball, Saussure had a daddy who was rich enough and so well-connected that young Ferdinand entered the world of European academia with little difficulty. Born in 1857, dead and buried by 1913 (which is prime), Saussure wasn't even that well known during his lifetime. He didn't publish much. In academic terms, most people would call him a complete nobody if it weren't for a pair of his dedicated former students/fanboys who decided to posthumously publish some of their late professor's ideas under his name in 1916. The book was called *Cours de linguistique général* and it reshaped how the western world viewed language.

Saussure's big idea: language consists of signs which we use to signify certain real-world objects and ideas and these signs are completely arbitrary. We speak, write, eat, and live in signs, which are just the sum of symbols and utterances (called signifiers) which we attribute to objects, people, and ideas (what's signified). In English we call those tall, woody things with leaves trees. In French they'd call those same objects arbres. The letters and sounds that go together to create these signifiers are arbitrary. Those same things could be called nipples and it would make as much sense as calling them trees. In Japanese, the kanji for those woody, leafy things is written as 木 (pronounced *ki*), which sort of looks tree-like, but the symbol could just as easily represent a man with an oversized penis. Nothing about *tree*, *arbre*, or 木 qualify them as signifiers for those woody things, but that's the reality we live in.

The pairing of each signifier with what it signifies is a complete crapshoot, but it's a crapshoot that society chooses to subscribe to. We decide by consensus what a word or phrase will mean. Like prime numbers, there's nothing inherently special about *tree* or *arbre* other than that we agree these words mean something. Each of us have our own linguistic quirks, but looming over us all is the grand structure of the language we all have to abide by. Language, as Saussure saw it, was as much a social construct as government or economics. We all have to come to some consensus on what words will mean and how they'll evolve. Language from this perspective is thus not so much a phenomenon to be studied as a social contract the linguist has to parse out.

In terms of how the world thought of language, 1916 was a pivotal year: Hugo Ball performed his sound poems for the first time, Saussure's ghost demonstrated how language might as well be sound poetry, the United States was on the verge of entering WWI, thus giving American soldiers the chance to corrupt the English of their British allies, and my paternal grandfather was born in a country where nobody spoke his mother tongue. The syllables Ball would proclaim on stage that year, those syllables that would prove so heavy they almost made him faint, may have contained secret words for *tree* or *phallus*, but it may have also contained the secret behind all human language, the key to achieving world peace, or simply a recapitulation of Saussure's theories. Or it could have been nothing.

Family History

Twenty years before Hugo Ball gave his reading at the Cabaret Voltaire, and seven hundred miles away from Zurich, a rabbi and his followers lived peacefully in a Czech village in the Austro-Hungarian empire, getting along swimmingly with the city's gentile population. But as with any group of people at any point in history, problems arose. The rabbi in question prided himself on being self-reliant, so the Shabbos was always troubling for him. He liked doing things for himself, and not being able to light his own fires or cook his own food frustrated him beyond belief, even if it was just for one day each week. He detested the idea of hiring a servant, so instead of hiring one he created one out of sod and wood. He wanted to create a golem, a monster made of inanimate matter that's brought to life by various holy and unholy means..

To bring his creation to life, the rabbi scribbled God's true, forbidden name on a piece of paper, rolled it up, and placed it in the mouth of the still-lifeless golem. The golem took its first breath of life, marveled at how filthy the rabbi's living room and kitchen were, and started cleaning and cooking for its master, no questions asked.

What was wrong with this? Nothing. The golem was happy, the rabbi was happy. The rabbi could survive the Shabbos without losing his mind and the golem got to enjoy six-day weekends. What was there to complain about? People found reasons.

The gentiles were creeped out by the golem, for one. The golem played with the children in the city, drank coffee and read novels at the local cafés. That shit just wasn't natural. And the city's Jewish community, while not as freaked out by the golem, still thought it was an abomination. The rabbi, a man of God, should have known better than to use God's true name for something so mundane. Who did this rabbi think he was, trying to own and use God's name like that?

So the Jewish and gentile communities of this quiet village decided the best course of action was to destroy the rabbi and his golem and forget any of it ever happened. And that was the end of the rabbi and his golem.

In that same community also lived an eighteen-year-old butcher's apprentice who would later become my paternal great-grandfather. At this time he was miffed at his dad for marrying a new woman after his mother had died, and watching his neighbors form an angry mob to raze a rabbi's house to the ground was enough to convince him that he needed to leave Europe as soon as possible. He decided nothing good could come of living here. So the next day he got in touch with local smugglers and, through a convoluted series of bribes, arrived in New York, then Massachusetts, followed by the West Indies, Peru, San Francisco, and eventually Casper, Wyoming. And on June 23, 1916, as Hugo Ball changed the course of poetic history, my great-grandfather's second wife gave birth to my grandfather.

Entropy and the Fate of Everything

There are three laws of thermodynamics, the last of which nobody can ever remember, so I'll join the consensus and skip it. The first two are easy enough to recall, though, and they're pretty important:
    Law 1: You can't create something (matter or energy) out of nothing.
    Law 2: Any system, no matter how large or small, will get hotter, messier, stickier, shittier, and just generally more fucked up as time goes by. In other words, entropy, chaos, whatever you want to call it, wins in the end.

The 1910s were a time defined by scientific discovery, with both the impossibly small and the cosmically large being busted wide open for the human intellect to explore. Physicists such as Niels Bohr and Ernest Rutherford proposed new models of the atom in 1913 (a prime number, as I mentioned earlier), and Albert Einstein published a paper on general relativity in 1915 (not prime). Quantum mechanics and the Heisenberg uncertainty principle wouldn't come on the scene until the 1920s, but the general fuckery of quantum mechanics (particles passing through solid matter, photons behaving as both waves and particles, electrons mutating from particles to clouds made of statistics) was alive in spirit throughout Europe. Franz Ferdinand had been assassinated, the old monarchies were on their way out, and now a bunch of nutjobs in Zurich were wearing masks and composing songs and poems in imaginary languages. It seemed that at any moment the world would end. The second law of thermodynamics was doing its work in the world and the world was in a panic.

As our species uncovered more of nature's secrets, we found ways to construct better weapons and thus better ways of killing each other. The more we learned about physics, it seemed, the more physics screwed us over. We knew too much and knew too little at the same time.

Drunk on Entropy

Everything I type now and everything you and I have ever read or written will be lost some day. That's just the shitty truth. Most of human history, literature, music, and culture is already lost and will be lost forever. Some of those forgotten epics and symphonies might have been masterpieces, but we'll never know. The world around us decays Tablets, canvases, and manuscripts erode and decay at random. Entropy is a stone cold son of a bitch when it comes to human endeavors. It simply doesn't care how good or bad something is. Through complete chance it will leave a beautiful manuscript to decay in one century and elevate Justin Bieber to popstar status a few centuries later.

Clay tablets, papyrus scrolls, and paper will erode with time, but our species has been clever enough to invent digital libraries to keep entropy off our asses for a little while. But those can hold out for only so long.

I can't repeat this enough: entropy doesn't care about us. Even if we invented a supercomputer dedicated to preserving every cultural artifact humanity has ever created, that supercomputer wouldn't be permanent. Eventually our species would go extinct, the way species always do. Our databases would outlive us for maybe a few million years, but just wait: one supernova or solar flare in the wrong direction and suddenly all that data will be corrupted. Letters will be scrambled and entire periods of history will be rendered unintelligible. Then entropy would just shrug its shoulders, laugh, and say, "Whoops, my bad."

Sound poetry fucks up this plan. Sound poetry is the tourist who always carries a wallet filled with Monopoly money and a piece of paper with "Go fuck yourself" scrawled on it just in case a pickpocket tries to steal from them. Sound poetry sees what entropy has in store for our species, our creations, the very idea of literature itself. Everything we've ever hoped for will be complete nonsense someday, so somewhere a sound poem is announcing itself as pure nonsense.

Entropy was in the middle of a dirty joke and sound poetry spoiled the punchline.

Graveyard Shifts

Not knowing a language will leave it dead before it reaches your ears.

I worked at McDonald's back in high school, a small-town McDonald's with a racist general manager and a staff in which I was one of the few white employees. It was miserable, but there was a camaraderie that blossomed between me and the international college-kid and immigrant enclave that can only arise when working a shitty fast food job.

Cut to two Marshallese women chatting to each other during a lull in business one night. I was salting fries, trying to make myself look busy, unsure if I was failing or not.

One woman (I think here name was Jenny) said something. A shocked, amused look spread across her face. The other woman, Margaret, developed that same look of shock, bemusement, and sudden realization. Then they couldn't control themselves. They laughed. Everyone else in the kitchen stared at them and we all wondered what the hell Penny had just said.

Any of us could have asked, but in a setting like a small town McDonald's, we tended to keep a friendly distance between each other, at least culturally. We were Nebraska Nice, often sharing knowing smiles and shrugs when we'd faced a rough lunch rush together or when one of us had experienced a nasty breakup, but when it came to asking specific questions about each other's histories and past struggles, we pretended those struggles didn't exist. It was too unpleasant. It was somebody else's business. Even though we could have developed a community we all needed at that point in our lives, whether we were getting ready to graduate high school or trying to adapt to a strange community in a strange new country.

Which was our loss. Penny had probably just delivered the ultimate zinger, the accidental joke to end all accidental jokes that had ever been uttered in the kitchen of the McDonald's in that small Nebraska town. And it probably didn't translate into English or any language but Marshallese.

That joke has a million graves now, all because of our unwillingness to bond with each other. It only survives in the tongue of a small island in the Pacific ocean. This is the ultimate curse of diversity, the wedge that culture and language drives between the members of our species. We lost a lot when Babel was destroyed. Too much became nonsense to our ears.

A Voyage to Finland

I've spent the night massacring a French dictionary by memorizing it. Maybe an overabundance of knowledge is just as deadly to a language as complete ignorance. You never know. Just as I'm about to fall into a well-deserved slumber, I realize I could easily murder Latin tomorrow. Why not? But then I remember that it's a dead language. How can I kill a language that's already dead?

Then I remember a trip to Helsinki I took during my senior year of high school, fully paid for by my dad's older brother. I took this trip with another fellow member of the debate team and a childhood friend who would soon take my virginity (but I didn't know this yet).

We arrived in Helsinki sometime in the beginning of winter, ate food that consisted entirely of unseasoned meat, weak gravy, and some undefinable purple jam, and learned to stomach the food by getting drunk at every possible opportunity. Somehow the three of us found a middle-aged woman willing to drive three American teenagers into the Finnish countryside for free that evening. Keep in mind, this was Finland. People expect teenagers to be stupid there, especially if they're foreign. Unlike in the States, adults in Finland revere the stupidity of the young.

So I found myself in the back seat of that lady's car with my childhood friend who would take my virginity that night. She had her window rolled down, smoking a cigarette. I asked her since when did she smoke? She said she'd never smoked before, not until this trip. My buddy from the debate team, the only person in our group who could actually speak an iota of Finnish, was chatting up the woman at the wheel, making her crack up with puns and jokes that probably didn't translate into English. I suddenly remember being jealous of every language that wasn't English at that moment, all the clever insults and dirty jokes I would never get to understand or create. Why couldn't there just be one universal tongue?

Suddenly the woman turned the dial on the radio. She landed on a station where a man was saying something that wasn't English and didn't sound like Finnish or any other language I'd heard spoken before. My buddy from the debate team straightened in his seat, amazed. He said something to our chauffeur and she laughed again.

I asked what was on the radio. My debate team friend said it was a 24-hour news station delivered entirely in classical Latin. And suddenly the rest of that trip is a drunken blur of lost virginities, nights spent in cabins, and my debate-team friend trying to teach me pieces of foreign and classical languages I still can't remember.

But I remember hearing Latin spoken for the first time, the v's pronounced like w's, the c's that were always hard. And then I recall that classical Latin, not just the Latin of the Catholic Church, is alive and well, no longer interesting or relevant but unkillable. I'll remember the hard, indestructible stuff of language. Latin found a way to survive, even if practically nobody understands it.

Confessional

I want to write a sound poem. I don't know if I can, but I want to make an honest attempt at it.

I imagine writing sound poetry is the kind of activity where making a deliberate attempt ruins the experience. Try it and you'll miss. Aim and you'll miss. I've talked to other poets about their disdain, fascination, or even admiration for this nonsensical form, but I have yet to meet a single poet who's written one. What are we all missing? What the hell is the secret?

I've asked Hugo Ball and I've asked Ella Fitzgerald (metaphorically, of course). I've metaphorically asked Mel Torme, but he never gives any straight answers. Then I (literally) asked a friend of mine who makes jewelry and he was surprised that sound poetry even existed. He claims he makes up nonsense poems and nonsense songs all the time when he's working or cooking. And of course I was jealous to learn this.

It's like abstract painting in verbal form. Sure, it looks easy, but anybody can say it looks easy. It takes a very special type of person to actually create something that looks easy and stick their name on it.

I'm occupying that disheartening liminal space between spectator and participant. I'm researching, reading, and writing about sound poetry, but so far I've come no closer to actually writing sound poetry. Where's the spontaneity? Why is it avoiding me? I know what language is made of, I understand the roots of sound poetry, I'm piecing together the religious and political aspects, but it's been a slow journey.

Maybe another anecdote will work. It doesn't involve a rabbie getting murdered, don't worry.

After divorcing my grandmother, my paternal grandfather spent a few years in the Philippines. He lived in a small house with an avocado tree growing in the backyard. He would have been poor in America with the small pension he'd received from his twenty-year stint as a parole officer, but in Manilla, every night was filled with endless drinks, endless women half his age and a third his weight, and all the fish and rice he could stomach. He became known as the White Man in Pink Sandals.

But one night, when he got too drunk and few women noticed him, he left one of his favorite bars early and drifted through the streets of Manilla singing nonsense songs to himself. Keep in mind, his Tagalog was terrible, and he was inebriated, so most of what he sang legitimately made no sense. But pretty soon he'd amassed an audience. Had the White Man in Pink Sandals lost his mind? Maybe. But my grandfather didn't mind how the world saw him. He performed for the old women and children who'd gathered around him and they tossed pesos at his sandalled feet. There was no sex or debauchery that evening, but he became a slightly richer man in more than just the literal sense.

Translation

Reading and listening to these poems has made me a translator against my will. This wouldn't be so difficult if I actually knew the language or if it even had a system of signification I could use. But that would be missing the point of sound poetry altogether.

Perhaps the greatest mistake our species ever made was assuming that poetry is united with words and their meanings. Back in the 12th century, Yang Wan-li realized the mistake we were making and tried to set us on the right path. "A good poet gets rid of words," he wrote. "If you say [poetry] is simply a matter of meaning, I'll say a good poet gets rid of meaning." Well,, what's left after words and meaning are stripped away? Yang Wan-li replied, "Get rid of words and get rid of meaning, and still there is poetry." I guess we just ignored him until the early 20th century. Sorry, dude.

The arbitrary grammatical rules we've all agreed to agree on are just that: arbitrary rules. We wanted to communicate meaning so we developed ways to construct and communicate that meaning. But these words and their messages are just masks for something we couldn't name or describe even if we attempted to. That unnameable, indescribable stuff is poetry.

I'm reminded of Ball's poem about a caravan of elephants, "Elefantenkarawane." No caravans or elephants are named, we don't glean any meaning about what these elephants are like or how they feel, but we find the flavor of elephants in Ball's nonsense. Ball achieved this without resorting to human language. He touched on meaning without meaning to mean anything at all.

What do we mean by pure poetry? Something that can't be put into words. So why bother with words at all?

If you want, go back to that chapter where I idiotically tried to analyze Ball's "Gadji beri bimba." I probably did a terrible job but that's only because I was trying to inject meaning where meaning wasn't needed. Tear that page out, insert a new one, and scribble your own interpretation of Ball's classic if you want. Chances are it'll be better than mine. Just remember to forget everything: grammar, vocabulary, syntax.

Reading and listening to a sound poem becomes an act of translation. The stuff of poetry, the stuff lurking behind the mask of language and Saussure's signifiers and symbols, emerges for anybody who leaves themselves open and vulnerable.

An Unnecessary Mining Allegory

This won't last long, I swear.

Imagine that poetry (not just the concept itself, but every line of poetry that our species has ever produced) is an ancient mountain range, the oldest in the world: the Black Hills of South Dakota.

A lot of people don't realize this, but there's actually gold in those mountains. Very, very little, but there's still some, and a lot of people have tried to mine it. It could have been any metal in any place on earth, but somehow we as a species agreed that gold is valuable. And since there's so little gold to be found in the Black Hills, we've agreed that Black Hills gold is somehow more special than other kinds of gold.

The mining process begins with a team dynamiting the hell out of a less-scenic part of the Black Hills, followed by the resulting boulders and rubble being transported by train to a distant processing center. There, the ancient granite is further bombed, ground down, and filtered until, for every ten tons of mountainside destroyed, a scab-sized flake of gold is extracted.

The gold is meaning, relevance, etc. The mountains are either ourselves or the languages we call home. It all depends on what you're looking for.

Twins

My father and his twin brother, Roger, were born on January 16, 1970, seventeen minutes apart. Nobody can remember which one was seventeen minutes older. My dad is still alive but my uncle Roger died on January 19, 1970. If he'd died at least three days earlier, he would have been considered stillborn. The labels are arbitrary. Time is fucked up like that.

There's no reason Roger should have died and my father should have lived. My dad could have died and I would have never existed. But because my dad lived and Roger died, we consider this sequence of events first and foremost. But it isn't hard to imagine my grandfather dying before conceiving my father. It isn't hard to imagine the entire earth being fried by a rogue solar flare before life had a chance to emerge. When time and randomness hold hands, watch out.

Anyway, there's some alternate timeline in which Roger and my father both survived. In this timeline, I like to imagine, they would have gained a reputation as those creepy twins who dress the same, eat the same things every day, and complete each other's sentences. They'd even develop a secret language between themselves that nobody else would know.

This language would be both communicative and performative. Roger would speak entirely in nouns, both concrete and abstract, while my father would restrict himself to verbs. Here's an imaginary transcript of one of their conversations:

Roger: Tooribah (translates roughly to Carmen Sandiego; Dad has no idea where she is or even where he and his brother or any of their descendants will be in the future)

Dad: Keekooqua (what two people do when they almost walk into each other in a hallway and one person tries to go one way, the other person also goes that way, and the two weave back and forth like pendulums until one person just walks around the other)

Roger: Gadji (literally "man in a Mr. Peanut costume"; any similarity to the "gadji" in Ball's poem is purely coincidental)

Dad: Lipsellum (pluperfect of "to be")

Roger: Hilaloo (eternity)

Dad: Capiterm (the act of ending everything; not necessarily suicide, more like hard-resetting the universe)

Masked Vigilante Justice, Pt. 2

There once lived a Belgian man named Adolphe Quételet who tried to pin down the average human form. Not ideal, just average. We're not talking about Plato's realm of ideal forms, in which everything from love, chairs, rabbits, to humans had a primordial, perfect form existing in some ether above and beyond our material world. This was the material realm in which the Average was divine. Ideal Man was no more. Enter *l'homme moyen*.

Or in English, the mean man, not mean as in pissy and aggressive, but mean in the statistical sense. Average every human being's height, weight, muscle and bone density, nose width, the distance between their eyes, hair length, the number of melanin granules in their epidermis, opiate concentration in their urine, etc., and eventually *l'homme moyen* will emerge from the data.

Out of the chaos of genetics and environmental influences, we can always count on a normal distribution for variables like height and weight in our species. There's a shape and order to randomness just as there's a shape and an order emerging amongst ourselves. So what if we kill each other in armed conflicts? So what if languages die? So what if we use written and spoken language to convince people to slaughter each other? That's just the will of the average human. There are bound to be a few wars here and there, a few master propagandists, just as there are a few giants and a few dwarves.

Taking inspiration from Quételet and his divine conception of mediocrity, I created a superhero alte-rego for myself in high school: Mu Man (alternately spelled μ Man). Named after the Greek letter that denotes the absolute center of the normal distribution, Mu Man was the embodiment of everything average. Never was there a more average superhero. With the intelligence of the average man, the strength of the average man, the stamina, speed, height, weight, and dexterity of the average man, Mu Man could do anything the average human being could do with the added benefit of wearing a mask and cape.

Though his career was short-lived, he racked up a few notable victories. He made a corrupt police officer in his hometown handle his dirty underwear, which also doubled as his mask at the time. That was pretty funny. But toward the end of his time on earth, Mu Man realized he needed to help humanity beyond humiliating public officials and protectors of the peace. But that's a story for another time.

A Definition of Deus ex Machina

In downtown Lincoln, Nebraska, in an abandoned shopping mall, is a bar modelled after a Prohibition-era speakeasy. The rules here are simple: no more than thirty people inside at any time, no texting or phone calls, no talk of modern technology of any kind, and all patrons must try their best to pretend they're living in the 1920s. You enter through a revolving bookcase which has no business in an abandoned mall.

 I'm here tonight to meet with a friend in the tech industry, who I'll refer to as M. M is a twenty-four year-old college student I met at an open-source software convention who spends most of his free time smoking weed. He claims to have connections with software engineers in Silicon Valley, the U.K., India, South Africa, pretty much everywhere. At one point he even crashed on Elon Musk's couch (allegedly). Never one to reveal too many details, he still claims involvement in most technology firms in the Midwest. He may be bullshitting, but I'll never know.

 I've already placed my order and all I can do is sit in semi-darkness on a plush chair, humming Dixieland jazz to myself, trying to blend in. I'm the only person in this place under the age of thirty. I feel claustrophobic. Bars shouldn't be this small, I think, and there should be more than one bathroom available.

My decision to hum Dixieland jazz to myself proves useless when Leo Watson's "Avocado Seed Soup Symphony" plays loud enough to distract me from my thoughts. It's not playing at an eleven or even a ten, but it's a solid seven, loud enough to disrupt any semblance of a peaceful, relaxed atmosphere. Plus, it's from the 1940s, not the 1920s. So much for historical accuracy.

M finally arrives.

"Sorry about the wait," he says. "I was Skyping with this guy from Calcutta."

An older couple a few feet away shoot my friend dirty looks. The woman is dressed as an aging flapper while her husband is dressed as Jay Gatsby if Jay Gatsby was balding and had a paunch. I wish they wouldn't look at us, but I can understand their annoyance: M, despite being the one who invited me here, is dressed and acting about as 1920s as a Def Leppard concert. We're sitting in a place where words like "cellphone" and "smartphone" are forbidden, and M's, dressed like a twenty-first century hipster and talking about Skype calls.

M lowers his voice to a whisper.

"What's with the outfit?"

He tugs on the sleeve of the oversized Zoot Suit I borrowed from my deceased, criminally rich uncle, the one who didn't die when he was three days old.

"I wanted to look . . . fly," I say, unsure if fly was an adjective in the 1920s.

The bartender gives me a sympathetic smile from across the room. He's in the middle of making my cocktail, some variation on a Manhattan that costs $15 more than it probably should. He lights then extinguishes a match over the tumbler, captures the smoke hovering over the cocktail with a slab of cork, then lets the smoke infuse with the drink for exactly two minutes.

"Period," M whispers. "I get it."

He leans back in his chair, takes a deep breath. He admires and smiles at a life-sized photograph of Babe Ruth hanging behind me.

"Let me just start by saying this," he begins. "What I'm seeking isn't so much the meaning behind the words but the full mask of the words. Do you get what I mean?"

I wonder if M's been blazing. It would explain a lot.

"No, I don't understand what you mean."

I get up to retrieve my cocktail and M follows me, hand on my shoulder, still whispering.

"I have this idea for a poem," M says. "But I'm not gonna write it. An algorithm will."

"That's been done before," I say.

"That doesn't mean it isn't worth doing again."

"I never said it wasn't."

"Who cares," M says.

We sit down again. M rubs his hands together, concentrates on the picture of Babe Ruth. He's too focused on sharing his idea to order something for himself. I glance over at the barkeep. He looks irritated.

"So get this," M says, "this program will read every IP address that currently exists, at every moment, and for each second for the rest of the Internet's lifespan, a new poem will be generated."

He's talking like his normal self again. Numbers, computers, terminology I have only the vaguest notion of. He stands somewhere between violating our most basic rights and achieving poetic greatness. He continues explaining as if I understand him, but of course I don't, but I still understand his premise: poetry from a machine.

"So what will this poem be about?" I ask.

"Nothing," M says, "it'll be complete nonsense. The true meaning is how it was made. This algorithm makes art by invading our privacy and it'll never stop. It'll be a monster."

I sip my smoky Manhattan. The smoky flavor is surprisingly nice, and for the first time this evening I feel like I can enjoy myself despite the cramped space and oversized suit.

It turns out M wants my advice. He knows I dabble in poetry. Maybe we could work something out? But then he turns the night into a nightmare. He pulls out his phone.

"Here, let me show you the code I have so far."

Gasps and angry glares from everybody. Especially the barkeep. He even drops a glass and lets it shatter for dramatic effect.

"Are you with him?" he asks. He's looking at me like I'm a 1920s time traveler expected to keep my 21st century companion in line.

"We're . . . hopping jazz, baby," I mutter. I'm ensuring my destruction little by little.

The barkeep steps from behind the counter and approaches us.

"Look, relax," M says, not helping anything. "It's just a smartphone."

"Smartphone?" the barkeep cries. Everybody else in the bar is silent now. "Smartphone!"

The barkeep repeats "smartphone," louder and louder until he's roaring.

"We don't say that fucking word here! Get the hell out!"

"Dude, relax," M says.

"Both of you get the hell out or I'm calling security!"

He's back behind the counter and positions his index finger over a large black button, threatening to press it.

"Leave," he says.

M almost objects, but I drag him through the revolving bookcase before he can make tonight any worse.

"Can you believe that asshole?" M says. We exit the abandoned shopping mall and are now in the heart of run-down, downtown Lincoln. "Over a stupid little word."

"Those are the rules. What did you expect."

M disagrees. For the rest of the night he abandons poetry to regale me with how the barkeep's a fascist, and maybe that's true, but more than I anything I marvel at the power the word "smartphone" had over him and how the power of that word was part of the same wheels-within-wheels system that included his power to press a button and sick security on the asses of anybody who pisses him off. Sure, maybe he was powertripping. But with Yahweh-like power comes a power trip. The nonsense M hoped to create and the arbitrary power of spoken language were more similar than either of us imagined.

It's Not What, It's How and Why

I wasn't lying to M when I told him there are poems similar to the one he was planning. I've even thought of creating one myself, but I've never had the time or technical knowhow to undertake it.

Nick Montfort's "Round" isn't a poem but an algorithm for calculating π. The algorithm starts at 3 and proceeds to calculate each digit from there. Each digit corresponds to a string of text, with a few line breaks thrown in for poetic effect. The note that accompanies the poem states that *Round* "is both non-interactive and deterministic." But it's not endless, even though π, an irrational number, is nothing but an endless list of random integers. In an ideal world, *Round* could be endless: a nonsense poem that could continue writing itself after the heat death of the universe. But entropy will win.

"As *Round* runs, the production of text will slow down as more steps are necessary to determine the next digit of π. Your computer will also slow down on other tasks and physically heat up," the note reads. See what I mean? Run this poem/program long enough and you'll witness entropy snaking its way into your corner of the universe.

Round wouldn't be a sound poem unless you read it aloud, in which case it would only evolve into a sound poem. Repeating the same phrases over and over again would lead you into that oral realm where, if repeated enough, any word can lose its meaning. But "Round" faces that disorder head-on and embraces it. This poem grips randomness and translates it into language that communicates not through words but by method.

The decision to create a poem like this (and let's not kid ourselves, we can't call this writing anymore) takes almost all the creativity out of poetry and confronts the reader and the programmer with language forced past its breaking point.

Compose a symphony based on patterns of cosmic background radiation. Write an epic poem without a plot, just assorted ingredient labels you find in your trash. Or do what Kenneth Goldsmith does and make the uncreative poem your specialty. Write poems that are nothing but autopsy reports or records of traffic violations. What you end up creating doesn't matter. It doesn't have to read well or even be readable. The intention, the fact that you chose to create something like this becomes the poem's meaning.

I've already mentioned I lack the technical skills to create something like *Round*, but I can always dream. I can meld it with sound poetry in my imagination.

My poem would involve chinchillas. Lots and lots of chinchillas, since I really like chinchillas. And thousands of keyboards hooked up to thousands of mainframes, all dedicated to storing the corpus that will be my magnum opus. I'd caffeinate those chinchillas and make them immortal if I could. And I'd want my mainframes to be immortal as well, even though I know that's as impossible as making chinchillas immortal. And the chinchillas would be free to roam the expanse of keyboards, eating, shitting, mating, and just generally living, each footstep they take becoming a character in an endless poem nobody will ever read in its entirety or ever hope decode or understand.

PART III

God Was Nonsense Before He Was Jesus

Performance

Maybe we're too used to poetry as a quiet, individual experience. You can blame sonnets and the Elizabethans for that. Live readings are the best way to experience certain masterpieces. "Gadji berri bimba," for instance. A close reading is pointless unless you've heard Ball himself reading it, or at least somebody imitating Ball. Dutch musician and sound poet Jaap Blonk performed the poem, along with five other Ball poems, in his 1998 album *Six Sound Poems by Hugo Ball*.

But Blonk's just one of the big names in modern sound poetry and surrealist music. You can't ignore the less renowned poets. When we were passing through Charlottesville, Virginia, one summer, my wife and I encountered a 6'4" man with a long red beard, a plaid shirt, and tattered jeans who called himself Joe Holmes. He sat at a typewriter, wrote poems and stories for tips, and sold self-published chapbooks of the verses and sketches he'd produced throughout his travels. He explained he was a street poet from New Orleans, a dying breed of writer mostly restricted to the American Southeast who sometimes migrated as far north as Baltimore.

My wife requested a poem about Canadian geese. Once he'd written it, instead of handing us the poem and letting us read it on our own time, Holmes insisted on standing in front of us and loudly reading the poem for everybody to hear. His poem (his voice) told the story of an American expatriate who found a golden egg and dreamt of cashing it in to live a life of luxury only to be attacked by an Amazonian band of female Canadian honkers.. My wife and I were flustered, but Holmes was long past self-consciousness. To him, each and every poem was an event worth announcing to Charlottesville, New Orleans, or whatever city he found himself in.

We all exchanged emails afterward, commiserated on the struggles all writers have to face, shared some drawings. I drew Joe a picture of a horrifying Canadian goose with wolf teeth, and my wife gave him a drawing of Kirby as a hipster.

This episode, this ritual, the moment in which my wife and I interacted with Holmes would have been meaningless without Holmes' performance. Exposing himself to the world, all six feet and four inches of him, with his typewriter, suitcase full of self-published chapbooks, and Polaroid camera was performance that had started as a hobby and morphed into a lifestyle. Pure Dada. Something that can't simply be seen, but something that must be lived and performed.

Nobody controls it. The *it* being poetic creation, the performance of a creation, anything connected to a creation. Not the performer, not the audience. Not just performing a poem or writing it. Prior to its creation, the universe conspired to bring the right people, the right time, the right locations and circumstances together to make all poems possible. Shit happens and we just happen to capture the shit. Maybe it's randomness, luck, or fate, but it's a phenomenon we have to respect. Joe Holmes put it best in his introduction to *Polaroid Potpourri*, his limited-run chapbook of selected poems he'd composed from 2017-18.

"A street poet shouldn't seek renown any more than a madwoman assigned to the oracle at Delphi on any given night," he writes. "We're just the medium on duty. Make of it what ya will."

How to Talk to Angels

If it seems like Hugo Ball kicked off this whole sound poetry thing, that's my fault, even though I tried to make it clear he was only sound poetry's stepfather.

Sound poetry goes back further than Ball. Take a look at any culture from around the world at any point in human history. I can guarantee that in some village, a shaman, priestess, or some other figure with a dangerous habit of dabbling in the metaphysical is either starving themselves or smoking/ingesting/licking some substance that will send them on what some would call a trance and others would call a bad trip. They see things, hear things, and will sometimes say things that a friend or neighbor will attempt to interpret. What are they saying? Who the hell knows. It could be bullshit. Or it could be a message from the gods, the greatest kimchi recipe in the world, a prophecy, or an encrypted warning about a future plague that will be spread through chinchilla saliva.

It's a phenomenon known as glossolalia or "speaking in tongues." Delphic oracles experienced it, and so have shamans in the Amazon and retired housewives in Pentecostal churches all across the Bible Belt. In the book of Acts the apostles experienced glossolalia for the first time when they were visited by the Holy Spirit. In the apostles' case, they weren't speaking nonsense but known languages, but despite this, witnesses at the event thought the apostles were hammered, insane, or some combination of the two.

Give it a shot sometime, chemically-assisted or sober. You might see God or you might see nothing but the floor and a mixture of your own vomit and tears. Either way, you'll rise from the noise hearing something unexpected. Just don't expect people to look at you normally ever again.

The Final Name

This is no longer a poetry of silence, suffering, performance, God, religion, or the Concept Formerly known as God (denoted by the Greek letter Omega or, alternately, a complete list of all prime numbers). This is the poetry of a language that refuses to die because it was never born. Before any conception of God, there was the Word (Logos) and that Word was so orderly, so chaotic, and so fucking unfathomable that simply putting it to paper would result in a document so massive it would create a black hole large enough to devour the universe.

Say it. I dare you.

Blasphemy is a theological curse jar. Say the wrong thing, tarnish the wrong phrase and the priest, after you confess your sin, will offer you a means of setting things straight with the Big Man. Just remember, the Big Man can get real mean. Just look what he did to the Tower of Babel.

You know you shouldn't utter certain phrases, but the fact that they're forbidden makes them enticing. Yahweh, I found out a few years ago, is just the Biblical equivalent of "frick" or "fug." The real, bonafide, true name of God in

Hebrew sounds like a combination of the name of a defunct online news site and a franchise of faux Mexican restaurants in Iowa. Say this word and you have to place your soul in the curse jar. It's a word so powerful that only certain people at certain times of the year at certain points in human history were ever permitted to speak it and survive. Sexy but dangerous.

    Say it. I fucking dare you, kiddo.

Don't Read This Out Loud

Say the wrong words and you'll wind up dead. What's in a name? A whole hell of a lot. It could hold a Rube Goldberg-esque string of events that leads to a baby grand piano falling off a truck roaring down an overpass that then falls on the hood of your puny Ford Focus while you're driving to work that crushes you to death. These things happen. Remember the story of the rabbi and his golem. Even writing a forbidden word can get you killed.

If you're lucky or if your heart's in the right place, the nonsense you mutter to yourself when you're tired might be nonsense, but it may be the kind of nonsense that contains the power to heal, forgive, or give thanks. It could also be a warning. After all, there's a pissed, Jupiter-sized elephant drifting in space somewhere waiting to devour our planet.

If we knew the actual names of angels, demons, and gods, life would be easier. We'd run no risk of killing or blessing ourselves just by babbling in private or when we're intoxicated. But life is never that easy. We're doomed to never know the true names of unknown forces. Remember that time you stepped on a Lego and you shouted some nonsense phrase instead of swearing like a normal person because you didn't want your mom to hear you drop an f-bomb? That nonsense phrase was actually the incantation to summon an ancient Cambodian chaos demon. Congratulations.

If you talk to members of certain Pentecostal churches, they'll tell you that glossolalia contains the most vital sounds ever produced by human mouths: the language of angels. The stuff they're chanting, the stomping, eyes rolling back in their heads: it's all part and parcel of speaking that language. Of course we can't understand it. How could we?

Ghost in the Word

Let's assumes this is the end of God. From now on, God is linguistic, a tip-of-the-tongue memory.

And let's assume we can huddle together with friends and lovers in Zurich, perform simultaneous dialogues, write sound poems, and dance and drink until we forget that time and Europe and Earth exist. Maybe that's world peace. Maybe that's what Dada and sound poetry hoped to achieve all along. Or maybe not. Maybe world peace will turn out to be a kimchi recipe or the taste of your favorite whisky. Maybe "world peace" is as arbitrary a term as "gazebo" or "Patrick Stewart."

Novelist N. Scott Momaday once warned that there's a man (or possibly woman) who possesses a word so powerful that, if they were to utter it, they could kill anybody they wanted to. He called this person the "Man Made of Words, but for accuracy's sake, let's call this deadly individual the "Person Possessing the Word.

I once heard from a friend of a friend of a friend of a former professor of mine that Momaday was bullshitting about the Person Possessing the Word. But I heard from another friend of a friend of a friend that the Person Possessing the Word was none other than Ella Fitzgerald. Another claimed it was N. Scott Momaday himself. We may never know.

God in the Machine

Arthur C. Clarke wrote a story in 1953 titled "The Nine Billion Names of God" in which a group of Himalayan lamas usher the end of reality, space, and time by using a supercomputer to print out all the possible, previously unknown names of God. The western engineers the lamas work with are skeptical, even patronizing of their eastern clients, but once every possible permutation of the forbidden holy name are printed by the Mark V supercomputer, the stars in the night sky start blinking out of existence. End story.

    The drunkard's walk, Brownian motion, or a horde of caffeinated chinchillas can work their magic to generate anything from God's possible names, poetry, or the complete works of Shakespeare. Given enough time, enough brute force, enough trial and error, perseverance can get you anything and anywhere. Maybe the universe is deterministic, maybe not. The fact remains, though, that a certain number of random movements of randomly situated molecules had to occur for life to emerge on Earth, followed by a slew of random mutations that gave natural selection the raw materials necessary to produce the bipedal, big-brained, war-waging species we all belong to. The random dance of genetics and evolution could have produced something different, but humanity is what happened. Language happened, and according to a lot of neuroscientists, our species' ability to speak and write may be just as genetically hardwired into us as our ability to make tools.

A different timeline could find Earth populated by colonies of tall, hyper-intelligent raccoons who speak a language similar to Hugo Ball's sound poems. I try to evaluate sound poems or computational poems through this lens of possibility. The meaning isn't hidden in the words but in how those words were made. Stand back from the words, squint, and you'll discover alternate realities, the disturbing truth that what we consider meaningful is arbitrary.

You'll find it in poems based on π. . You'll find it in blasphemy Name a god and you're supposedly laying claim to that god. Said god will be pissed. Said god will then kill your ass or put a premature end to the universe. But some gods are also words. Some people are irrational. Some people are prime numbers. Some gods are the Word.

Poetry as Prayer

Let's forget there are any tensions between art and religion for a moment. Let's forget about American Puritanical Christianity™ sucking out all the poetic verve Christianity used to have. After all, there's an entire book in the Old Testament that's an erotic poem. Never forget that.

Poetry, whether it's a psalm, a prayer, *Paradise Lost*, T.S. Elliot namedropping philosophers in a failed followup to *The Wasteland*, or a Lucille Clifton poem about menstruation or post-9/11 America, is a form of prayer.

After cutting ties with American literary icon/douchebag David Foster Wallace, poet Mary Karr decided to give the Catholic Church another shot after a long spiritual hiatus. She came to know God through and as poetry. Prayer is a poetic act and poetry is a religious act. Just meld the two together and we're closer to understanding this whole God conundrum. She didn't even need to abandon poetry the way Ball did.

So an American poet prays in the back row of a Cathedral. A jazz singer scats herself into ecstasy and forgets what time tastes like. A German poet/playwright swoons on-stage on the evening of June 23, 1916, and has to be escorted off the stage as if he caught a glimpse of God's face. Call it prayer, call it glossolalia, call it nonsense, call it sound poetry, it doesn't matter. It all points in the same direction. Keep walking, you won't miss it.

Riddle #2

Q: What's the difference between divine intervention and a hot jazz number?

A: The singer.

PART IV

Scatland Utopia

Sweet Music

Louis Armstrong invented scat in 1926 when he and his band were in the middle of recording "Heebie Jeebies" and Armstrong dropped the lyric sheet he was supposed to read from. Rather than take things from the top, Armstrong was struck by ingenuity and a general sense of not-giving-a-single-fuck and proceeded to sing whatever syllables and sounds popped into his head. And thus scatting was birthed carelessly into the world. Or at least, that's one account of what happened.

If there's one place the influence of sound poetry can be felt, scatting is perhaps the most obvious. It's just sound poetry set to jazz. And like sound poetry, the art of scatting can be deceptively simple.

Just as there's a right and a wrong way to sing opera, there are right and wrong ways to scat. There are techniques to master, patterns and phonetic vocabularies to recognize and employ, and a history of improvisation to draw from.

Enunciation is a good place to start. If you can't babble clearly, why babble at all? And you can't forget purpose: what musical instrument do you hope to imitate?

The blare of the trumpet, the thumping heartbeat of the double bass, the pleasured moan of the trombone, or the seductive wail of the tenor sax? You need to make a choice. And let's not forget improvisation, the difficult art of making shit up as you go and finding a way to make it sound like music. It's more science than art. Doctors of music (the high priests/doctors of jazz) have written entire theory and practice books dedicated to teaching prospective scatters the proper techniques and strategies. They've even developed iPhone apps to pass on the sacred art.

Did I call it sacred? Of course it is. I don't think it's a coincidence that Mel Torme once called Ella Fitzgerald the High Priestess of Jazz. Prior to the 21st century, musicians knew how important their music was to the state of the world's collective soul. Talk to any jazz musician and they'll talk about it like it's a religion, a religion that's arrived just in time to save us all, a religion that defies human definition and thus needs sax, piano, and scat solos to explain its eschatology. And when you get really in-depth with them, they'll discuss jazz the same way an astrophysicist will talk about the inevitable death of the sun and our solar system. It's equal parts linguistics, music, God, and chaos theory.

First Lady of Song

It's 1938. Ella Fitzgerald has managed to work her way out of homelessness and starts performing with the Chick Webb Orchestra. She records "A Tisket, A Tasket," a reworking of a nursery rhyme that, according to who you ask, gets the original lyrics dead wrong in some cases (Fitzgerald says the basket is brown instead of green), but she interjects a hot scat solo, which shows she's onto something revolutionary.

She's singing bebop, which, believe it or not, was a controversial genre at one point. She becomes the First Lady of Song, which begs the question of who exactly she's married to, and whether the President of Song can scat with Fitzgerald's range and prowess.

It's 1940. It's 1950. Ella Fitzgerald's manager forces her to wear a blond wig for a concert in Las Vegas.

Later, she wants a television show of her own, even if it's just a local show in New York City, but she can't get her own show. No matter how talented Fitzgerald was, a white audience just couldn't stomach black skin on television at the time. That doesn't keep Fitzgerald from fantasizing, though.

The show Fitzgerald imagines would feature her and her fellow musicians, guests, and the warm, fuzzy feeling that she's inviting you, the viewer, into her home, or maybe you're inviting her into your home. It doesn't matter who's the invitee. The result, the feeling, the sense of closeness would be identical. And Ella and her band could play a song, first fast, then slow, and see which version sounds better. And if they mess up the number, well, that'd be just fine and dandy, that would be right ducky. They could start over, just like in real life, away from the rampant perfectionism of the recording studio.

It's now 2019 and Ella Fitzgerlad is truly the journalist's nightmare. Enough articles and interviews have been collected that you could tell any story you wanted about her. Fitzgerald locked her personal life away, only sharing it with close friends and family. But sometimes she would open up. Maybe she wouldn't be completely honest about herself, but she provided the kinds of details that tell us more than a life history ever could.

Her story goes like this. It's 1972. It may have been Detroit, it may have been Las Vegas, or it may have been Kansas City. On stage, she was scatting like she'd never scatted before, even though she'd just had cataracts surgery and, according to some, her voice was beginning to falter. But she scatted nonetheless, going low, going high, twisting around rhythms like a serpent around the branch of a dying tree. And when the song ended the audience applauded, all except for one woman seated near the stage. Fitzgerald noticed her despite her failing eyesight. The woman was scowling.

"What's wrong?" Fitzgerald asked. "Didn't you like the music?"

"The music was alright, but I couldn't understand a damn word you just said," the woman replied.

"Well, let's sing you something you *will* like."

And Fitzgerald performed her take on Marvin Gaye's "What's Going On." And the entire audience, including the unhappy woman, applauded after Fitzgerald and her band finished. Even though Gaye's song is supposed to be a protest song, Fitzgerald never performed it as one. To her it was music, poetry, a feeling, something more permanent than protest. Some resented her for this. Most people didn't seem to mind.

Synch, Pt. 1

I have synchronicity and spontaneity stuck in my head. So much of what goes into any act of creation, whether we're talking about the creation of universes, galaxies, apple pies, or poems, hinges on a string of lucky coincidences.

Inspiration should be banned as a concept. Inspiration implies that creativity happens suddenly, usually just in time to give the artist their magnum opus.. Which is a pretty narcissistic way to look at art. The universe, God, the muses, whatever or whoever you worship when you're trying to paint or write, don't exist to help you. They might care, but I bet 90% of the time they want you to figure shit out on your own. Nothing comes premade or pre-packaged.

Joseph McHale, a painter I know, says most non-artists never understand this. They think art is coin-operated in some cases. A woman in the office Joseph works at once asked if he could paint her a picture of a cow. Not an inventive or unconventional painting of a cow, but the kind of picture of a cow you'd find by typing "cow" into Google Images. She thought artists could just create anything on-demand without thinking things over first. But it's slow work, Joseph told me. Most paintings, even if they're abstract, can take up to half a year to complete. And even when new ideas strike him, they're never delivered by the gods. The brain of the artist is a stable where ideas are cooped up and allowed to grow antsy before you finally have no choice but to set them free. What feels like sudden inspiration is really a festering idea finally surfacing.

Take that allegory about mining for gold in the Black Hills I wrote earlier, for example. It felt like it came out of nowhere, but after I wrote it I remembered learning about how gold is mined in the Black Hills back in fifth grade. Nothing new. It was just my memory venting. Who knows, maybe my mind will shoot out a sound poem pretty soon.

A Séance

Again, this is just one version of the truth.

My wife and I once held a séance. Well, we didn't hold or conduct it, we just hosted it. A medium we know through a friend of a friend actually oversaw and did the real work while my wife and I just did what the medium said. All the medium requested for her troubles was a bottle of wine.

Our medium had just finished half the bottle of Chardonnay I'd given her and made us sit in a circle around our kitchen table, which is very difficult due to our table being rectangular. The medium permanently reeked of German potato salad, which was pleasant for all of five minutes. And she had a death grip. Seriously, I couldn't feel my right pinky for a week after she let go of it.

"We know you're here, spirit," the medium muttered. She burped then laughed.

Nothing yet. My wife shot me a look that said, "Are we really going to go through with this bullshit?"

Then we heard it.

"SKAbadabadabadoobelidabbelydabbladabbladab-blabBELibabBELibabBELibabBELabBELodooBELiboDO."

"What was that?" I asked.

"Quiet," the medium said. She cleared her throat, preparing to address the spirit directly. "Tell us your name, spirit."

"I'M THE SCATMAN!"

"What's your purpose here?"

"This has to be a joke," my wife said.

"Quiet!" the medium screeched. "I need absolute silence from both of you." Addressing the spirit again, "Are you the one they call the Scatman?"

"Wanna sing a song with me?" the spirit asked.

"I can't sing. Sorry," the medium said.

"Everybody stutters one way or the other," the spirit replied.

"Understood," the medium said. "Why have you come to us? What's your purpose?"

"Repeat after me."

"Repeat what?"

"Repeat after me."

"Repeat *what*?"

This continued for about twenty minutes. Whatever Scatman John (or Scatman John's ghost) wanted, the medium wasn't able to provide it. Or maybe the Scatman wanted me or my wife to say something. I don't know.

I have no way of explaining what occurred that evening, but what we summoned may have just been a ruse by that drunk medium or Scatman John's actual ghost. Maybe we'd caught Beelzebub in a strangely jazzy mood. I won't lie, I secretly hoped we would get in touch with my dead uncle Roger. But Scatman John wasn't the worst ghost to discover.

Scatman's World

If part of your solution isn't ending the pollution, then I don't want to hear your stories told. I want to welcome you to Scatman's world. I'm calling out from Scatland. I'm the Scatman. Tell me about the color of your soul. Scatman, fat man, black and white and brown man. I sit and see and wonder what it's like to be in touch. Everybody's talking something very shocking. Because while you're still sleeping the saints are still weeping, because the things you call dead haven't yet had the chance to be born. In other words, stillborn.

I'm lifting everything I can from John Paul Larkin, an American jazz pianist and vocalist who moved to Germany and became the superstar known as Scatman John in the mid 90s. It's not *Scotland*, it's *Scatland*, a land created and popularized by Larkin where everybody lives in perfect harmony with each other, regardless of color or gender, humanity and nature coexist in perfect harmony, and everybody speaks Scattish, a language which may or may not feel like sex in its spoken form.

Against my will, Larkin has morphed into the central figure of everything I've written so far. He had the vision, the nonsense, and the religious zeal that can only come from a healthy dose of disillusionment and wishful thinking. He scatted and dreamed utopia.

But before music, Larkin was just a stuttering boy who endured years of bullying because of his speech impediment. *Everybody stutters one way or the other* and Larkin had it worse than most people. When he took up the piano in his early teens he finally found a way to express himself that didn't involve struggling to get from one phrase to the next. As a jazz pianist, there were only his hands, the keyboard, the recording studio, the audience, and his band members. Eventually he started scatting and singing over his piano. He never stuttered then. Most stutterers rarely stutter when they're singing (or when they're angry).

He took to cocaine and alcohol. His wife despaired over his health, but Larkin carried on. Nothing can stop the Scatman. Except for America and its lack of enthusiasm for jazz.

So he abandoned America and the American dream. He attended stutterering support groups, got sober, moved to Hamburg, Germany, and through sheer random, dumb luck landed himself a record deal with an executive who had the crazy idea that Larkin's scat singing would mix well with the exploding Europop craze.

These were the foundations of Larkin's new church: scat singing and the (hopefully) transformative power of music. Already in his mid-fifties, he became a popstar. America didn't seem to care for long, but Germany and, surprisingly, Japan loved him. Especially Japan. And Japan loved Scatland, that realm of uncorrupted language, uncorrupted people, and uncorrupted landscapes. Like Ball, Larkin saw the nonsense coming from his mouth as a species of divinity, an unknowable set of instructions that could save the world if we would just unironically believe in it the same way Peter Pan and some indie musicians unironically believe in fairies.

It sounds like kid stuff, but that's because it is. Can you think of anything better?

Teenage girls in Europe and Japan screamed his name, sometimes swooned over him. He loved this, but not for the obvious reasons.

"The whole thing behind Scatman," Larkin said, "is that I don't put out stuff that says kill a cop or overthrow a country. I put out positive stuff."

The Word as light. Ignorance as darkness. Suffer the little children. The Word being unintelligible and unknowable to human ears and minds until the proper moment. Yadda yadda yadda. Scaddilydiddlybeebopbo.

Riddle #3

Q: What do you get when you cross a hot jazz number and the inevitable heat death of the universe?

A: Hugo ball peering into the future.

PART V

The World's Turning Like a Sundial

Synch, Pt. 2

When I tell people I'm writing this book the conversation soon turns to whether I'll write a sound poem. And I doubt I can, even though I want to. Or maybe I don't want to and don't realize it yet. Maybe my creative process isn't spontaneous enough. Joe Holmes, the street poet I met in Virginia, seemed to revel in spontaneity. But he didn't seem to think he was writing those poems himself.

"A street poet shouldn't seek renown any more than a madwoman assigned to the oracle at Delphi on any given night. We're just the medium on duty," he wrote. Maybe he's right. Maybe if I want to write a sound poem, I'll have to wait for that perfect moment of inspiration, a moment that will arrive outside of myself. The resulting poem will be my creative stepchild.

One of my mom's cats died recently, hit by a car. This was the same day the cat of a bookstore owner in Lincoln, Nebraska, died. Her customers were all in mourning. Over five hundred miles between the two cats and their owners, yet a single day and a common fate joined them. I learned about their deaths on the same day, within the same hour.

I keep convincing myself this coincidence means something, but maybe it's the kind of meaning you find in a scat solo or "Gadji berri bimba."

Butterfly Bullet Without Wings

Hopefully we've come closer to that boundary that lies between language and the stuff we call poetry. The specific words and grammatical rules are just the clothes we drape over the big ideas which in turn conceal the animal hiding beneath it all. Language ends, poetry begins. Yadda yadda yadda.

I'm currently in bed with a 103.7 degree fever listening to *Democracy Now* on my city's local radio station. That Canadian doctor who got shot by Israeli soldiers a few months ago is being interviewed. He recites the same set of facts I've heard about Gaza since 2004: a small, contested nub of land that rests under centuries of religious, ethnic, and historical tensions; Israelis v. Palestinians; Judaism v. Islam; a conflict with no end in sight; U.N. sanctions; condemnations and oaths flying every which way. The same news story, song, and drama we've all witnessed for years.

Then the doctor says the Israeli armed forces are using butterfly bullets against Palestinian protesters, and suddenly the conflict changes. The world changes, in fact. At least for me.

Butterfly bullets (sometimes called dum dums), as the doctor explains, are bullets that detonate and blossom into deadly, tissue-tearing flowers of shrapnel when they hit their targets (people). The doctor says Israel may have been using this type of artillery against Palestinians (both military and civilian) since as early as 2013, but who really knows. There's so much speculation and hearsay that the truth no longer means anything.

As I hear this I don't know what to think. Has a new technology suddenly developed while I remained ignorant? Actually, no. Exploding bullets have been around for over a century, I soon discover after a quick Google search. Apparently the Hague outlawed them in international warfare way back in 1899.

Maybe it's the fever, maybe it's the sudden paranoia, maybe it's the unhealthy amount of weapons and military research I suddenly find myself steeped in, but I'm on the verge of some historical revelation.

A little over a century separates us from WWI and the birth of Dada. Back then people would have been horrified to hear accounts of troops being ravaged by mustard gas and improved artillery, wondering just how destructive technologies like that could go unnoticed for so long by such a large segment of the world's population. They would have likely wondered what science and technology had been up to when they weren't looking. Were they all asleep? One moment science and technology were humanity's greatest allies, making locomotives faster and unlocking the secrets of gravity and quantum mechanics, then they were dissolving soldiers' lungs and transforming meadows into fields of craters and dismembered limbs.

And here I am, feverish, bedridden, hidden away in a midwestern university town that might as well be Zurich it's so insulated from the world's ruthlessness. Every WWI veteran is separated from our time by death and decay, but Earth's kept spinning and revolving, and humanity has kept the same game going for another century. I wonder if I should write a poem about this. But when has a poem ever solved a problem? Hugo Ball and his cohorts tried that a century ago. The hippies tried it. My friends and I are trying our best to try it. But what could this really accomplish? The only thing that's changed is the time, but the planet is still the same planet, and the years seem to be repeating themselves. How many of those years will be prime? I wonder.

I'm part of that hot coffee and cappuccino crowd, the kind of yuppy who attends poetry open mics, listens to and supports public radio, and shops only at local grocery stores. I'm the kind of yuppy who's now trying to convince himself that acknowledging I'm one of humanity's lucky few is enough to absolve myself.

But absolve myself of what?

A New Definition of Trauma

Maybe the Police put it more succinctly in "De Do Do De Da Da Da." Sometimes the logic of language escapes us, seems useless, maybe even ties us up and metaphorically rapes us. Often, when we've seen some shit, we just need time to vent and spout enraged, grieving nonsense. Or maybe Cathy Park Hong said it better yet when she wrote, "When a poem becomes commemorative, it dies." It doesn't matter what's being commemorated or mourned. Pin down the trauma and the mourning and any poetry that might follow is lost. Aim and you'll miss it.

Enter the unofficial *grande dame* of sound poetry. She was known simply as The Baroness, Elsa von Freytag-Loringhoven. Her poem "Neele Hülcker - Klink Hratzvenga" is an attempt to distill the very essence of the grieving process, a distressed wail, into noise. Take a look:

nARin — TZARissAMAniLi (hE is DEAD!)

Ildrich mitzdonja — astatootch Ninj — iffe kniek —
Ninj — iffe kniek!
Arr — karr —

Arrkarr — barr Karrarr — barr — Arr —
Arrkarr — Mardar

Mar — dóórde — dar — Mardoodaar!!!

Mardoodd — va — hist — kniek — — Hist — kniek?
Goorde mee — niss — — —
Goorde mee!!!

Narin — tzarissamanilj — Narin — tzarissamanilj!!!

Hee — hassee? O — voorrr!

Kardirdesporvorde — hadoorde — klossnux Kalsinjevasnije — alquille — masré Alquille masréje paquille — paquille Ojombe — ojoombe — ojé — — — —

Narin — tzarissamanilj — Narin —tzarissamanilj!!! Vé — O — voorrr —! Vévoorrr —

Vrmbbbjjj — sh —
Sh — sh — —
Ooh!!!
Vrmbbbjjj — sh — sh — Sh — sh —

Vrmm.

    The poem's opening line reads, "ARin — TZARissAMAniLi (hE is DEAD!)" which is easy enough to unpack. The all-caps indicates that AR, TZAR, and AMA are meant to be screamed aloud, as if wailing certain parts of a departed's name. I assume (and this is only in my head since the poem itself is pure nonsense) that the speaker's dead loved one's name is something along the lines of Arin Tzariss Amanili, or maybe Tzara himself, and he/she/they may have been both a tzar and a man. The constant use of em-dashes I interpret as sighs or sobs racking the speaker. I like that. I should use that sometime.

What does the intervening nonsense hope to convey, though? It's a mystery, but the eighth stanza signifies a major change in how the nonsense presents itself to the reader. Whereas earlier the sounds sounded distinctly German, this stanza presents sounds resembling Greek and Latin. I don't know, "klossnux" seems pretty Greek. And the phrase "alquille — masré Alquille masréje paquille — paquille Ojombe" strikes me as the closest arrangement a sound poem can ever achieve to Cicero's Catilinarian orations.

The wail dies down toward the end. Shhhh, shhhhh, shhhhhhhhhhh, shhhhhhhhhhhhhhhhhh*hhhhhhhhhhhhhhhhh*. Like that. Just like that.

"Vrmm." That's a silent, resigned sob, a silent acceptance of the Lord givething and the Lord takething away if ever I've read one.

The Saving Grace of Scattish

I once knew a girl who belonged to a Pentecostal church, the kind of church where babbling, whether sincere or not, is regarded as the highest form of prayer. If you couldn't speak in tongues, you weren't favored by God. So there was always pressure to conform and perform, to show off the linguistic gifts the Heavenly Hosts had decided to bestow on you and your family, even if they were bullshit.

This girl (and it wasn't just this one girl, keep in mind, there are plenty of children born into the folds of these churches who are subjected to similar experiences) had a mother who was obsessed with proving to the world, and especially her fellow church members, that her family was truly Touched, the epitome of holy rollers. So when her daughter finally reached the age of ten and still wasn't speaking in tongues, the mother worried. To save her daughter's soul, she locked this girl in a closet for an entire day, informing her that she wouldn't be released until she spoke the language of angels.

"And if you don't speak the language of angels, well, you'll wind up in Hell," her mother said.

Hell was cartoonish in this girl's mind. Hell is cartoonish in the minds of plenty of children, people who, when they're that young, don't understand that Hell as portrayed on television is just a fantasy whipped up by Dante Alighieri to get back at his IRL enemies. So she was scared of the idea of Hell, not Hell itself. But more than anything she just wanted out of that closet. She cried, tried to calculate how long it would take before she depleted the oxygen in the closet and how long it would take for her to starve to death. People died this way all the time, or at least that's what she thought.

She saved herself (don't ask me which part, though) by caving in to her mother's demands. She babbled loudly and wildly. Overcome with joy, her mother threw open the closet door, praised the Lord, and hugged her child. This girl kept babbling for her life, unsure when or even if she should stop. She didn't want to be forced back *in there*.

Talking like a baby delivered her from a subspecies of evil. Just what this form of evil was remains uncertain. We can call it an abuse of power. The stronger subjugating the weaker members of society can manifest itself in many ways: violence, silencing, legal and economic sanctions, declarations of war. The possibilities are endless. The truly deranged powers of the world can turn on you seemingly at random. There's no safeguard against randomness other than randomness.

Childhood's End

The big names of Dada are all dead. Ella Fitzgerald is dead. John Paul Larkin is dead. Every WWI veteran is dead. An entire (living) chapter of our planet's history is lost. At some point we need to acknowledge that our younger, happier days are over.

But we can try to relive them. Ilia Zdanevitch (who went by Iliazd in print) was barely old enough to remember the halcyon days of Dada, but still hoped to capture those miracles in a bottle by publishing the collection *Poesie de Mots Inconnus* in 1949 (another year which happens to be a prime number). He printed this conglomerate of sound poems, simultaneous dramas, and abstract art on only the highest-quality paper, dividing each page into quadrants to get the most love and content into each sheet.

He divided this collection as much as possible, as if fragmentation can become a genre if you believe hard enough. The "poesie" in the title is printed as "poe sie." Even the year of publication is rendered as "An 1919 et 30," as if Iliazd desperately wanted to stave off 1920 for just one more year and allow the Dada party to rage on for just a few more wild nights.

You'll find all of Iliazd's heroes here. Ball, now a corpse, offers sound poems that look even more encrypted and entrenched in the unknown than "Gadji beri bimba." Hausmann, Tzara, even Pablo Picasso make appearances as both visual artists and poets.

You'll find love poems, dramas, lamentations, and dances depending on how you look at things. Ronke Akinsemoyin invites the reader to place a cupped hand over their mouth like a valve and imitate a biplane taking off, whirring through the air, and shooting an enemy biplane. "L'attaque des caimons de la solde" by Antonin Artaud unfolds like a drama in random syllables, featuring a cast consisting of a choir, birds roosting in a tree, the tree itself, the god of war Mars, a casualty of war, and the corpse of a general. But I like to imagine he's not just a dead general, but General Death. Every drama needs some kind of supervillain. It makes life easier to stomach.

I could explicate each poem, and I'm sure Iliazd would have appreciated my enthusiasm. But the only one left was Iliazd at that point. The people who wrote those poems were, by 1949, either dead or had moved on to other projects and other parties. And here was Iliazd, with his grand ambitions, his artisan paper and wood prints, wondering where the hell everybody had run off to.

Some Key Historical Events: 1916-2001

1916: Hugo Ball gives his most famous performance at the Cabaret Voltaire. My paternal grandfather is born. H.P. Lovecraft publishes "Dagon." A man in Cambodia gets killed by a falling coconut instead of discovering any secrets of gravity. James Joyce is living in Zurich and may or may not have attended the Cabaret Voltaire during its heyday.

1922: The Irish Civil War begins. James Joyce publishes *Ulysses* in its complete, non-serialized form. One section, "Sirens," features Leopold Bloom trying to write a letter in the middle of a loud pub. Language becomes nonsense. A shattering dish and the ring of a bell take on the cadence of human speech.

1923: The Irish Civil War ends. The Kanto Earthquake hits Tokyo. King Tutankhamun's tomb is discovered and, according to some metaphysical radicals, so is his curse.

1927: Hugo Ball dies. Fritz Lang releases *Metropolis*. A baby who will later become Pope Benedict XVI is born in Marktl, Germany.

1938: Kel-El becomes Superman. Ella Fitzgerald records "A Tisket, A Tasket."

1942: Paul Celan (not his real name) is placed in a Romanian concentration camp.

1945: Paul Celan (not his real name) survives long enough to escape said Romanian concentration camp alive. He goes on to become the world's unofficial Poet of the Holocaust, a permanent witness to the century's most heinous acts. Despite his title, however, he never resorts to mentioning Hitler, the Nazis, or even WWII by name. Sometimes language can't commemorate trauma.

1949: Iliazd arrives late to the party with *Poesie de Mots Inconnus*. NATO is born, as are boxer/grill salesman George Foreman and novelist Haruki Murakami.

1951: A year which happens to be a prime number. The largest prime number known in this year is $(2^{148} + 1)/17$.

1955: Ray Kroc opens his first McDonald's in Des Plaines, Illinois. Six months later, the USSR tests their first two-staged H-bomb, the RDS-37, over modern-day Kazakhstan.

1962: Peter Parker is bitten by a radioactive spider and becomes Spider-Man for the first time. KMart is born and Walmart births itself from the ashes of the 1950s.

1969: Donald Burdick publishes *Tongues: To Speak or Not to Speak*, an introduction to glossolalia for American

Christians wary of dabbling in holy babbling. Bryan Adams claims to have an unforgettable summer during this year.

1970: The Beatles disband. Casey Kasem launches the radio show *American Top 40*. Richard Nixon calls for the U.S. invasion of Cambodia.

1975: The Vietnam War (or Vietnam Conflict depending on who you ask) ends and the U.S. pulls out of Cambodia. Spain's Francisco Franco finally kicks the bucket.

1980: John Lennon is assassinated. Mt. St. Helens erupts. The Police release "De Doo Doo Do De Da Da Da."

1985: *Ripley's Believe It or Not* features a segment on sound poetry, during which Marie Osmond reads Ball's "Elefantenkarawane." Coca-Cola releases New Coke™, which may or may not have been brilliant self-sabotage.

1995: John Paul Larkin, now going by Scatman John, releases "Scatman's World." *Mother 2* is released in the U.S. as *EarthBound*.

1998: Composer and sound poet Jaap Blonk releases "Six Sound Poems by Hugo Ball." *The Legend of Zelda: Ocarina of Time* is released.

2001: *Pootie Tang* is unleashed on the world. The film's titular character is "too cool for words" and his speech is a hybrid of nonsense and pure sex appeal. In addition, a couple guys hijack a couple of planes, and now a couple of buildings are missing from the New York City skyline.

Masked Vigilante Justice, Pt. 3

When we last saw our hero, he was in the middle of making a corrupt small-town police officer handle his dirty laundry. With his hometown now safe, Mu Man sets his sites on preventing every world tragedy that's ever happened. But how?

He needs to go back. To the beginning of it all.

Using his average powers, Mu Man drinks himself into a coma in order to travel back in time. As a side-effect of the whiskey he just consumed, which was blessed by a Scientologist water filter salesman (see *The Average Mu Man,* Vol. 10, Issue 7) he's not only able to travel backwards in time but shrink down to the size of a thymine molecule (the average size of all physical bodies in the universe, coincidentally).

Now no larger than an organic macromolecule, Mu Man finds himself in a puddle of primordial ooze. It's unbearably hot, everything smells like fermented durian broth and fish, and our hero suddenly develops a craving for Malaysian food. But now is no time to eat. Losing no time, Mu Man finds the nearest chain of molecules in the ooze conspiring to coalesce into DNA.

"Heheheh," cackles one chain of nucleotides. "Let's get this show started."

"You bet, adenine," a fat, ugly molecule of guanine says. "Let's implement our nefarious plan. Let's start life!"

"Not so fast, evildoers!" Mu Man declares.

"Mu Man!?" a stabilizing phosphate cries. "How is this possible? We haven't mutated enough to create humans yet."

"True, but I have my ways," Mu Man says. He smirks. "Remember that water filter salesman who tried to mutate you to create a hybrid of L. Ron Hubbard and Johnny Carson? Well, he provided me with a pint of whisky so powerful it not only allowed me to travel back in time to kick your asses, it's also allowed me to shrink down to your size."

"You think you can stop us?" the stabilizing phosphate says. "We're gonna fuck over this planet whether you like it or not."

"Fucking over people who don't even exist yet? That's low, even for you," Mu Man says. "Why not try picking on somebody your own size?"

[Continued in *The Average Mu Man*, Vol. 16, Issue 9]

It's Impossible to Be Completely Truthful

Sound poetry's creation story is one of escapism, hope, rebellion, and linguistic liberation. But in all its uncertainties, distortions, and gaps, the story has to be filed under that tricky category of "mythology." The stories I've retold, paraphrased, distorted, or invented may not all be entirely true, but they point toward something larger than the individual stories themselves. A Word created the universe, but words, through unforeseen chains of events, led to propaganda, warfare, mass destruction, genocides, etc. Then a few people tried to strip language of its meaning to redeem the world, and what resulted was glossolalia, sound poetry, scat singing, etc. It goes by several names. Each version is just one part of the truth.

    A rumor is born. That rumor grows legs, starts spreading through a major city, and eventually worms its way into enough people's conversations that it becomes a possibility. Then that possibility becomes a full-fledged tale and climbs its way up the ladder of plausibility until it's history.

Or maybe it becomes a fairytale. It doesn't matter much these days. The Internet can make anything seem plausible and lead people to believe even the most ridiculous stories. We live in times when a rumor can become a fairytale, grow wings and evolve into a myth, then continue to fly up the ladder of plausibility until it surpasses history and becomes common knowledge.

There's despair here. But there's also redemption and maybe a bit of grace. Maybe there's hope, too.

What follows might be the sound poem I hoped to write when I first undertook this project. It might be a story about meeting God after discovering Him in a string of prime numbers. It could also be a set of instructions for assembling an atomic bomb, the secret to world peace, or the perfect kimchi recipe. There's no right, wrong, or even possible interpretation or translation because there isn't one.

There's nothing here and there never will be. There's nothing here except for the party.

PART VI:

----k-k-eee-yyyyyyfff

kalalalala ---- groooooolapalapalapalapa lapalapalapalapala

          mell pell pill pill pull pull ----
creeeeee
EEEEEeeeeeEEEEEEEEEE
           freeeeeEEEEEEeeeeeeee

pilpil – pitpitpit ----------------------

cosgorro tillibiliustimidibitimus eros
asquaguavarame durioburronavne
pluriburius furrorvorius craplop

torrotorro torri torri
kim cop plurrrrrrrrrr----

simsimsimsim
sinsin sin sin sin
shhhhhhhhhhhhhhhhHHHHHHHHHHHHHHHHHHHhhhh

ooooooooooOOOOOoooooooo
o o o o o o o o

ABOUT THE AUTHOR

Lane Chasek's stories, essays, and poems have appeared or are forthcoming in *Broke Bohemian, Contrast, Hole in the Head Review, Jokes Review, Lincoln Underground, Paragon, Plainsongs, Sheila-Na-Gig,* and others. They were the winner of both the 2016 and 2017 Laurus Poetry Prize, and their essay "Becoming Vegan in Western Nebraska" was the featured nonfiction selection in the anthology *Voices of Nebraska: Diverse Places, Diverse Peoples* (University of Nebraska Press, 2016). Besides writing, Lane enjoys watching 90s horror movies and cooking plant-based Sichuan recipes.

Printed in Poland
by Amazon Fulfillment
Poland Sp. z o.o., Wrocław